PRAISE FOR
BECOMING BRAVE

"Romans 8:28 is one of my favorite scriptures—especially when I find myself going through the inevitable times of trials that always result in the strengthening of my faith. You know, the painful 'molding and shaping' sieges that God allows in His infinite wisdom and love for each of us to grow us up in Him for His purposes and glory. The Word of God is my ultimate yardstick for truth and direction, but then there are those rare books that come along that are written from the heart to edify and encourage the body of Christ. *Becoming Brave* is one of those books that will affirm we are not alone and to bravely press on, in Jesus' mighty name!"

—**JENNIFER O'NEILL**, actress, author, speaker

"Henry David Thoreau was right when he said, 'The mass of men lead lives of quiet desperation.' The truth is, most of us fail in life because we simply do not dream big enough dreams. If that's your affliction, then Tracey Mitchell has the cure. Her new book *Becoming Brave* is a challenge to entertain the impossible. It's about confidence in yourself and trust that God has a far bigger plan than you ever thought possible. This isn't the time to *give* up—it's the time to *rise* up and become everything you're called to be. Get this book. You'll never look at life the same way again."

—**KATHLEEN COOKE**, cofounder of Cooke Pictures and The Influence Lab; author of *Hope 4 Today: Stay Connected to God in a Distracted World*

"*Becoming Brave* is a modern-day field guide for the woman who wants to overcome. Whether you are struggling with a personal habit or a devastating loss, Tracey Mitchell can show you how to get back on your feet and fight with courage. She presents a practical, faith-filled battle cry to every one of us who have experienced weakness, disappointment, or even despair. Are you ready to live above and beyond what's happened to you and live your life in a way that embraces courage, ignites dreams, and demolishes fear? Then this book is for you."

—**JAN GREENWOOD,** author of *Women at War*; Equip Pastor, Gateway Church

"Tracey is one of the most genuine and unpretentious people I know. She has an authoritative and respected insight into the Word of God. Tracey is an amazing teacher—a powerhouse of knowledge and a motivating force. In a world where fear is rampant and the world and society as a whole placate it, medicate it, and give in to it, Tracey's book *Becoming Brave* will light the pathway of ending the crippling stronghold of fear. Take the journey with her and embark on the voyage to freedom and fulfillment."

—**JULIE A. NOLAN,** president, TCT network

"*Becoming Brave* is a call to revisit our Bible-based beliefs and to demonstrate them by our behavior—even when there is not even a glimpse of a light at the end of the tunnel. Tracey's wisdom is motivating and will add value to the lives of all who read this anointed book."

—**DEBORAH SMITH PEGUES,** TV host; bestselling author, *30 Days to Taming Your Tongue* (more than 1 million copies sold)

"Every season of life brings with it the opportunity to fall into a cycle of fear. If we are not equipped to recognize, confront, and conquer issues that would seek to strip away our confidence, we will soon lose sight of our dreams. *Becoming Brave* will help you rediscover your voice and find your footing as you courageously move forward in faith. Open its pages to discover the source of courage and healthy self-identity."

—**THELMA WELLS**, DD, Women of Faith,
international speaker, author of 41 Books

"A must-read for all women who want to think big, dream wild, and live free of fear. Tracey's book will encourage you to step outside yourself to see a bigger picture. She will encourage you to move from just surviving to thriving."

—**DR. TRUDY SIMMONS**, host and executive
producer of *The Christian View*

"As a fellow overcomer of the destructive forces of abuse and their effects on one's personhood, I lock arms with champions like Tracey Mitchell. Her timely book *Becoming Brave* will nudge you to the edge of your fears where you can safely face them and leap into your destiny with the faith and assurance of your belonging in Christ, equipping you to become all that you were created to be!"

—**BRENDA CROUCH**, author, speaker, TV cohost

"Tracey Mitchell's *Becoming Brave* is what I would call a 'necessity-read.' Growing up and living in Norway, Scandinavia, I've learned the importance of becoming brave. I discovered fearless living is not an attribute we are born with but something we choose to become. Tracey Mitchell is far more than the author of this book—she is a living example of Becoming Brave. This powerful read will take your thinking and dreams to a bold new place."

—**EDWARD JOHN HUGHES**, *Scandinavia
Today*, TV host, recording artist, author

"*Becoming Brave* is no journey for sissies. It may well be the toughest road you'll ever travel. But Tracey Mitchell provides an excellent road map from your valley of fear to the peak of courage you hope to attain. Through her poignant personal story and vulnerability, in *Becoming Brave* Tracey teaches us how to move from fear and failure to fearless and conquering. So lace up your running shoes and join Tracey on the journey of a lifetime—the hope-filled road to becoming brave, the life-altering trip from here to heaven. Read it and reap!"

—**MARY HOLLINGSWORTH**, bestselling author; president and publisher, Creative Enterprises Studio

"This book is real and authentic, addressing issues women deal with in life. Thank you, Tracey, for imparting your life experiences and giving women the tools to do all God has called us to do. You are truly helping women."

—**SANDY SCHEER**, copastor of Guts Church, founder of Guts Girls

"Fear schedules intimidation, manipulation, and domination, resulting in the incarceration of your dreams in a prison of failure and regret. *Becoming Brave* by Tracey Mitchell is a fear destroyer and imparts master keys to unlocking your dreams and soaring with new confidence and success. Implement the revelation in *Becoming Brave* and your impossibilities will become mission accomplished!"

—**DR. MIKE BROWN**, author, master mentor, founder and president of Strength and Wisdom Minisries

"*Becoming Brave* is full of powerful tools to be used against the tactics of fear, doubt, and discouragement in everyday life. This book will equip you for growth as you learn to live out your God-given destinies through faith in Christ!"

—**SABRINA HARRISON**, coowner of MINT dentistry, founder of Equipped by Faith Ministries, interior designer

"Tracey Mitchell's book *Becoming Brave* will open your eyes, equipping you to step out of your pain and into your future. In each chapter she communicates with inspiration and compassion, showing you how to break free from shame, pain, and blame. You will discover how to love yourself, forgive those who have hurt you, and live without limitation or fear."

—**DON CLOWERS**, pastor, crusade
evangelist, author, conference speaker

"*Becoming Brave* is profoundly on point when it comes to igniting, reclaiming, or rediscovering courage. It exposes the lies the enemy would have us believe in order to defeat us and keep our dreams paralyzed. After reading this book you feel empowered to conquer the things that have undermined your confidence. Tracey eloquently brings truth to what becoming brave really looks like for the everyday Wonder Woman—the one who doesn't wear a cape but is a world changer and doesn't even realize it. A brilliant read with tools and insight that will make you want to become brave."

—**WENDIE PETT**, fitness and wellness
expert, TV show host

Becoming
BRAVE

BRAVE

HOW TO THINK BIG, DREAM WILDLY, AND LIVE FEAR-FREE

TRACEY MITCHELL

EMANATE
BOOKS

Published in Nashville, Tennessee, by Emanate Books, an imprint of Thomas Nelson. Emanate Books and Thomas Nelson are registered trademarks of HarperCollins Christian Publishing, Inc.

Thomas Nelson titles may be purchased in bulk for educational, business, fund-raising, or sales promotional use. For information, please e-mail SpecialMarkets@ThomasNelson.com.

Unless otherwise indicated, Scripture quotations are taken from the New Century Version®. © 2005 by Thomas Nelson. Used by permission. All rights reserved.

Scripture quotations marked ESV are from the ESV® Bible (The Holy Bible, English Standard Version®). Copyright © 2001 by Crossway, a publishing ministry of Good News Publishers. Used by permission. All rights reserved.

Scripture quotations marked AMP are from the Amplified® Bible. Copyright © 1954, 1958, 1962, 1964, 1965, 1987 by The Lockman Foundation. Used by permission. (www.Lockman.org)

Scripture quotations marked GW are from *God's Word*®. Copyright © 1995 God's Word to the Nations. Used by permission of Baker Publishing Group. All rights reserved.

Scripture quotations marked ISV are taken from the International Standard Version (ISV). Copyright © 1995–2014 by ISV Foundation. ALL RIGHTS RESERVED INTERNA-TIONALLY. Used by permission of Davidson Press, LLC.

Scripture quotations marked KJV are from the King James Version. Public domain.

Scripture quotations marked THE MESSAGE are from *The Message*. Copyright © by Eugene H. Peterson 1993, 1994, 1995, 1996, 2000, 2001, 2002. Used by permission of NavPress. All rights reserved. Represented by Tyndale House Publishers, Inc.

Scripture quotations marked NASB are from New American Standard Bible®. Copyright © 1960, 1962, 1963, 1968, 1971, 1972, 1973, 1975, 1977, 1995 by The Lockman Foundation. Used by permission. (www.Lockman.org)

Scripture quotations marked NIV are from the Holy Bible, New International Version®, NIV®. Copyright © 1973, 1978, 1984, 2011 by Biblica, Inc.® Used by permission of Zondervan. All rights reserved worldwide. www.Zondervan.com. The "NIV" and "New International Version" are trademarks registered in the United States Patent and Trademark Office by Biblica, Inc.®

Scripture quotations marked NKJV are from the New King James Version®. © 1982 by Thomas Nelson. Used by permission. All rights reserved.

Scripture quotations marked NLT are from the Holy Bible, New Living Translation. © 1996, 2004, 2007, 2013, 2015 by Tyndale House Foundation. Used by permission of Tyndale House Publishers, Inc., Carol Stream, Illinois 60188. All rights reserved.

Scripture quotations marked NET are from the NET Bible®. Copyright © 1996–2006 by Biblical Studies Press, L.L.C. http://netbible.com. All rights reserved.

Any Internet addresses, phone numbers, or company or product information printed in this book are offered as a resource and are not intended in any way to be or to imply an endorsement by Thomas Nelson, nor does Thomas Nelson vouch for the existence, content, or services of these sites, phone numbers, companies, or products beyond the life of this book.

ISBN 978-1-4002-0810-4 (TP)

ISBN 978-1-4002-0811-1 (eBook)

Library of Congress Control Number: 2018943348

Printed in the United States of America
18 19 20 21 22 LSC 10 9 8 7 6 5 4 3 2 1

For our brave, beautiful children

You are braver than you believe,
stronger than you seem,
smarter than you think,
and loved more than you know.

—A. A. Milne

CONTENTS

FOREWORD

As I can attest, the world can leave us battered, hurt, and feeling fragile. But we are to be more than our doubts and insecurities lead us to be. I know what it feels like to be at the end of your rope when all you want to do is survive until tomorrow. Instead of throwing in the towel and giving in, we should fight!

In my friend Tracey's book, *Becoming Brave*, you will find an encouraging message about how to be restored and renewed by the power of God in the midst of all the pain life throws at you. It is not easy to live as a woman of God in our pain-filled world. Tracey provides real tools to help us deal with hard questions about being faithful and living as a godly influence when chaos strikes. The enemy desires nothing more than to leave us so worn down that we have nothing left with which to encourage our sisters in Christ or to stand as a strong beacon for God. Use this incredible book to either find your way back to a fiery desire to declare victory or simply to find out you are not alone in the fight.

Becoming Brave will show you how to handle your faith when it conflicts with the world around you. But it also teaches how to strengthen and reassure your sisters in Christ. Even if life has dealt you an unjust hand, through God you can claim victory and move from surviving to thriving. God has a plan for us that is greater than the suffering we may endure and the attacks the enemy brings our way. Ladies, we are empowered women of God! I pray Tracey's words remind you—as they did me—of the bravery and courage available to us when we refocus our eyes on Jesus.

Tracy Strawberry
Strawberry Ministries

chapter
ONE

JOIN THE RANKS

You would have enjoyed meeting my friend Beth. Everyone did. Warm, loving, easygoing, she made the world a better place. Her love for life and people was infectious. She had a gentleness about her that made life seem less complicated, more enjoyable.

Late last fall I received a text from Beth. She would be traveling through Dallas on her way to Georgia and asked if we could connect. Eager to visit, I made plans for us to have lunch at a corner bakery. It had been more than six months since I had seen my friend. I was overjoyed by the thought of spending a few hours laughing over memories and catching up on the details of our lives.

I arrived at the bakery a few minutes early and scanned the crowd to see if she had grabbed us a table. My eyes bounced around the restaurant. No sign of Beth. Then I heard a soft, familiar voice say, "I'm right here." The voice and smile belonged to Beth, but the sunken, skeletal frame bore little resemblance to the rosy-cheeked friend I knew. My expression must have mirrored my fear. When her bony frame hugged me, she whispered, "Don't worry; it's going to be okay." I felt a wave of nausea sweep over me as I steadied my emotions to receive the news.

Stage 4 non-Hodgkin's lymphoma. The words roared in my ears. My mind struggled to comprehend what the diagnosis might mean. Her recent bouts of fatigue, low-grade fever, bone pain, and weight loss were all cancer related, her oncologist had confirmed. Apart from a miracle, six to nine months was the best she could hope for, given the prognosis. Later that day, Beth took a flight to a cancer treatment facility in Atlanta. That was the last time I would see my friend.

I've often wondered, how different would we live each day if we knew our days were numbered? What would happen if we knew the exact date we were going to die? How would we react? Would we sit silently and try to hold on to each moment? Would we dig through our nightstands, searching for that bucket list of things we never got around to doing? Would we drown in a sea of self-pity? Or would we do what my friend Beth did the last few months of her life and bravely encourage others?

Beth did not view cancer as an enemy but as an opportunity: an opportunity to comfort the widow in the hospital room three doors down, whose family was unable to be with her during her final weeks of life. An opportunity to share encouraging words with a staff member going through a devastating divorce. An opportunity to celebrate her roommate's remission—a favorable prognosis—the same day she herself was given devastating news. In the midst of life's most challenging moment, Beth rose above the crushing physical and emotional waves of cancer. She didn't just look for ways to escape her pain. She searched for ways to encourage others in theirs.

God is looking for more Beths. "Sheroes" disguised in leggings and hoodies rather than tights and capes. Wonder women who care more about their sisters than about themselves. The greatest moments in life are when we have the courage to ignore our own needs and instead reach out to the hurting around us.

Cancer isn't the only situation that requires courage. You may not be fighting for your health, but you may be facing bankruptcy, a family rift, the ending of an unhealthy friendship, a miscarriage, or the unexpected loss of a loved one. You are not alone. Life is not always easy. Heartache is real and pain is often unavoidable. But your response to unexpected crisis will determine whether you sink beneath or rise above the waves of chaos. The truth is, crisis reveals who we are.

Seated in a worn leather chair at my favorite Starbucks, I pay attention to the women around me. I see what makes them tick. I look just as closely at the woman whose four-inch stilettos click crisply across the floor as I do at the sister who flip-flops her way to the counter. One carries a tan designer bag; the other, a thin vinyl backpack. One wears short, manicured nails; the other, chipped blue polish. Different worlds? Obviously. Same heartbreaking issues? Most likely.

I've spent countless hours listening to women share their private stories of grief. My heart breaks for the twenty-five-year-old who tearfully describes how what she'd *hoped* would be a happily-ever-after love story ended abruptly. My pulse quickens when I hear disturbing tales of unexpected betrayal, gut-wrenching heartache, and controversy. It's hard to hold back tears when I see the fallout of unfulfilled promises, smeared reputations, and innocent victims needlessly dragged through the minefield of life.

Although each woman's story is unique to her set of circumstances, there is one common thread in all our stories. In the midst of our pain, our hearts wonder, *How do I find the courage to get through this?*

Let's be honest. Life can get messy. No one plans on her marriage turning into a nightmare, but it happens. Detours intersect with our paths to happiness. Discrimination exists. Inequality is real. Cancer. Divorce. Unfaithfulness. Abuse. They all happen. We discover life isn't as carefree as we imagined. The world isn't as safe as we once thought. We try to make wise decisions and keep an optimistic outlook. Then along comes one of those sucker-punch moments, and our lives are irreversibly altered. Sometimes they are the result of another person's dysfunction; often they are the repercussions of our own choices and actions. But how we react when the world throws a dagger at our backs determines whether we will become victims or survivors and thrivers. Will we buckle under the pressure, or will we pick up our swords and fight for our joy, our peace, our families, our *future*?

Becoming Brave is for any woman who would courageously choose the latter over the nagging voice in her head urging her to slip into her flannel pajamas and hide beneath the covers of doubt and discouragement.

Maybe just hearing the word *chaos* or *crisis* makes you want to run the other way. I beg you to reconsider. We will never conquer life's most pressing problems until we are brave enough to address our issues. We will also never reach our dreams or fulfill our destinies.

Pain is no respecter of persons. We could swap stories on how we've fallen apart during life's darkest seasons. I will be the first to admit I've had my share of meltdowns. But I've learned that the enemy only gains great ground when we bury our hearts in our insecurities or take cover beneath the security blanket of denial. That's a false security. Refusal to face life's greatest challenges does not dissipate the storms; rather, it empowers them. I have seen people whose lives were in shambles dive headlong into a bed of depression, only adding to their troubles. Conversely, I have observed others, with equally pressing problems, stand their ground, raise their shields of faith, and declare victory. Their courageous resolve in desperation transformed their worst moments into their finest hours.

A victorious life is not stumbled upon; it is cultivated. It's the result of choosing to be bold, brave—*fearless*—when everything in you wants to cower in defeat. If you are serious about defeating the things that seek to destroy you, you must decide to be fabulously fierce and face your problems head-on. And you must tackle these difficult questions:

- Am I willing to trade my best days for a life spent wallowing in the pit of unrealized expectations?
- Will I permit the claws of injustice to strip me of my God-appointed destiny?
- Will I enthrone feelings of loss, empowering them to steal my peace?
- Will I waste my life grieving over those times when I was blindsided by hurtful situations?

A victorious life is not stumbled upon; it is cultivated. It's the result of choosing to be bold, brave—*fearless*—when everything in you wants to cower in defeat.

- At the end of my days, will I look back with embarrassment and realize that I authorized feelings of failure to snatch the joy right out of my life and to derail me from pursuing my dreams?

You don't have to agree to any of these things, but it is *your* choice.

I am confident we women can dry our tears, lift our heads, double our fists, and come up swinging, fearlessly confronting every challenging situation and recovering what has been lost. In fact, I am certain we can emerge stronger and wiser when we learn to rise victoriously above our experiences, not just survive them. So in this book I'm going to challenge you to bypass the quicksand of self-defeatism. It's a consuming pit, one that is hard to escape, but I promise to steer you away from the lies of the enemy, who seeks to convince you that you're disqualified from receiving God's favor or blessings.

As an encourager of women, I make it my job to expose the seductive schemes that would pull the plug on your joy and peace—and your future. Nothing makes me want to hurl my coffee cup across the room more than seeing someone full of potential fall victim to the spirit of frustration. I refuse to let you go out this way.

I decree that you will not stay paralyzed and powerless. Grief, loss, and devastation will not consume you. Acts of betrayal, slander, and injustice stand no chance of derailing your destiny. And bitterness and burnout will be dethroned as you stand your ground and face life with confidence and assurance.

I've waded into emotional sinkholes to help people learn how to pull themselves up and out. Together we've cried, laughed, debated, and prayed for clarity. Through every counseling session, I've sought biblical understanding and God's wisdom and discernment. But before I could help anyone else, I had to spend many days and sleepless nights challenged by my *own* fears and pushed far beyond the safe haven of my emotional comfort zone. Forced to confront my own share of insecurities, doubts, and fears, I have grown stronger and now walk in renewed confidence. I've learned how to rise above circumstances that once threatened to wear me down. You can too.

My process toward becoming brave and resilient has been a spectacular journey, unlike anything I've ever experienced. My tears, fears, smiles, and secrets are woven throughout each chapter. I pray you will come away from this book with a new perspective and the courage to embrace life in an enthusiastic, passionate, and eager way. Together, and with God's guidance, we can rise above any situation that threatens to wear us down. We can learn to think big, dream wild, and live fear-free!

Think big, dream wild, and live fear-free!

What do you say? Are you ready to stretch into a new season? Then join me as we *entertain the impossible* and begin our journey toward divine courage and confidence.

FOR

Further Reflection

1. How different would you live each day if you knew you only had *six months* to live? Would you embrace the time you have left and leave a lasting legacy, or languish in regret over how you've lived your life thus far?

2. Think back over your life. How have you helped others while facing trials of your own—or have you? Are you there for others even when you're suffering your own heartache? If not, who do you know that could use some moral support? How can you provide that support?

3. Often, crisis can help us understand more about who we are. What have you learned about yourself from the crises you've encountered? Can you identify any positive character qualities that you developed during adversity?

4. In which area(s) of your life do you feel most discouraged? Relational? Financial? Career? Or something else? How are you preparing to rise above what threatens to wear down your faith?

chapter

TWO

WIRED TO BE
BRAVE

Tap. Tap. Tap. Her black, strapped heels clicked across the polished floor. As she gently swayed to the music, her low-cut evening gown hugged her figure in just the right way. She was Manhattan's resident *it girl*. The kind of woman men try to trap and women try to tame. Some people are born stunningly beautiful. Chloe was that lethal combination of brains *plus* beauty. A familiar face within New York City's social circles, Chloe ranked high on the list of *must-have* people at your party. A resident of the wealthy Upper East Side, she filled her days searching for the latest fashion trends to arrive from London. At night she floated between dinner parties, red-carpet events, and premieres. Envious? Don't throw her under the bus just yet.

Chloe is a fictitious name. Her story is real, but her true identity is *Agent 355*. No, I'm not talking about a Bond girl. Agent 355 was one of Washington's most trusted spies during the Revolutionary War. Brilliantly brave, she slipped secrets from Britain's highest-ranking officers into the hands of the American commander in chief. It was the inside edge the colonies needed to topple the world's most powerful military. To this day, no one knows the identity of Agent 355, a reminder that it's often the no-names who rewrite destinies.

I can't promise that if you're brave, your memory will be inscribed in a history book. But I can promise that brave women always change the course of history. Maybe silently. Perhaps slowly. But their influence will definitely alter the trajectory of someone else's journey. You don't have to live the salacious life of Agent 355 to experience the ripple-effect reward of being brave. I know women who have changed the course of history from their tiny prayer closets, coffee nooks, country walking trails, and urban lofts. The fact is, most women don't realize they are changing history while they are changing diapers or washing out bedpans.

And they don't know they are hardwired to be history makers.

During the past year, I have been on a journey of discovery of sorts. I have endeavored to identify what sets apart truly brave women from those boisterous women who only appear brave. I think I've about nailed it down and hope to have it neatly outlined for you in this book.

Taking a hard look at what it means for a woman to *become brave* has unnerved me in more ways than I can share in one sitting. When I started out on this journey, I thought I had the subject matter locked down already. After all, I have been studying our gender through the microscope of Scripture for decades. I vainly imagined I had a pulse on all our strengths and vulnerabilities and knew exactly what a courageous woman was made of. I didn't. The truth is, I was forced to lean in, look deeper, and get gut-level honest. Not only did I have to dethrone the images of some of the women I once held in high esteem, I also had to tear down any lofty ideas about my own courage.

That required more nerve and transparency than I felt comfortable with.

More than ever, I'm convinced most of us have deep insecurities about how we would respond if our faith and fears were to collide. We try not to go there. Impulsively we try to wash away *any* negative thoughts before they have time to grow roots. We glance at our newsfeed and cringe when we see the picture of a precious four-year-old with tubes coming out of her nose. We halfheartedly type, "My prayers are with you." But for the life of us, we won't take five minutes to imagine the agony that child's mother must be going through. If we did, perhaps it would change how we pray. It might even change how we engage.

Let me own up to some of my own indifference to those who are suffering. Just last week, on my way to the airport, a homeless man stood on a busy corner, rattling coins in a dirty plastic cup. It was easy for my hands to reach for spare change but impossible for my heart to imagine, *What if this were me?* I tried for a moment, but the memory of growing up underprivileged myself made me shut down. I dropped the quarters in the cup and the accelerator to the floor. Does that make me shallow or mark me as insensitive? Well, it certainly wouldn't land me in the ranks of the brave.

No matter how brave we want to imagine we are, life will eventually call our bluff. An MRI machine whirls around our heads. A homeless family looks us in the eyes. We become foster parents of defiant twin teens. And for every opportunity to become brave, a dozen voices will try to cripple our confidence. Those voices don't whisper; they scream. They call to us in our weakest moments, whether through an accusing email, a close friend's betrayal, a rebellious teen, a drunk ex-spouse—the invitation to discouragement is endless.

After trying to reconcile my fears and my faith, I've come to this conclusion: if I am to have even a *remote* chance of bravely facing down my fears, I'll need to knock back a few stiff shots of courage. So will you.

It's time we drink up.

Thirty-five minutes behind schedule. Ugh. Ashley had zero chance of making it to work on time. She hated to burn a vacation day so early in the year. Especially after Christopher hinted that a marriage proposal might be in their future.

She toyed with an imaginary timeline. Engaged by April. Wedding in early December. A two-week honeymoon in Hawaii. *Honeymoon* . . . That was a warm thought she could wrap her aching body around. Thoughts of the crystal blue water and sandy beaches took her away . . . till someone called her name.

"Ashley? Ashley Anderson."

A gruff-looking nurse scanned the room, searching for acknowledgment. Slowly, Ashley grabbed her belongings and stood up from the waiting-room chair. Seeing her, the nurse turned and headed toward the examination rooms. Ashley trudged after her. The door closed behind her.

"Step up, please." The nurse gestured to the oversized scale in the corner. Ashley obediently stepped onto the scale. "Up three pounds from last time. Step down and take a seat . . . That's right. Now, open up." She slid a thermometer into Ashley's open mouth. "Hmm . . . 98.4."

Ashley experienced a momentary brain freeze. Was 98.4 high or low?

"Bathroom's down the hall on the left, and cups are on the back of the commode. Get me a urine specimen, and place your cup on the shelf when you're finished."

Ashley disappeared down the hallway and entered the sterile restroom to render the urine sample. She emerged to find the nurse waiting for her.

"Ready? Follow me this way."

They went down a different hall and entered a patient room.

"Take your clothes off, put on this hospital gown—ties in front—and have a seat," the nurse instructed. "The doctor will be in to see you soon."

The door clicked shut and Ashley plopped down on the room's one chair. Her legs bounced impatiently as she picked up an outdated gardening magazine and flipped through it. *Gardening. Who has a garden in Soho?* Five minutes passed. *Time to scroll through Facebook.* Ten minutes. *I'd better text the office and explain to Marla why I'll be a no-show.* Fifteen minutes. Finally, Dr. Karn tapped on the door.

"How are you feeling?" he asked as he entered the room.

"More tired than normal, like I have the flu."

"How's your appetite?"

"Not good. Occasional nausea."

"Flu cases have been unseasonably high in uptown. Have you been out of the country?"

"Two months ago I spent a weekend in Tahoe."

The word *Tahoe* made her flush with excitement—and guilt. It was there she and Christopher had spent their first weekend together. The memory pricked her conscience. She had known better than to tempt her passions in such a romantic hot spot. Her moral compass opposed sexual relations before marriage. But between the mounting pressure of her company's new merger and her mother's recent diagnosis of early-onset Alzheimer's, she'd caved at the idea of a carefree weekend. Less pressure, fewer responsibilities . . . perhaps Dr. Karn would agree that she needed that again and demand a few days' bed rest.

"Chance of pregnancy?"

Instinctively her mouth formed the word *no*, but just before the syllable left her lips, the gravity of that possibility sank in. Her face turned white and her hands felt clammy. Unconsciously, she pulled the thin waiting gown tightly around her midsection.

"Well?" he said impatiently. "Any chance you are pregnant?"

"Umm . . ." Ashley dropped her gaze and picked at a fingernail. "Well, I . . . I don't usually . . . My boyfriend and I . . ."

"I see. Sit tight a sec. I'll be right back."

Ten minutes later, Dr. Karn confirmed her newly formed fears. "Pregnant. Seven weeks along. I'll send someone in to explain your options."

Pregnant. Unbelievable. Forty-one and pregnant. How could I have let this happen? For crying out loud, it was a weekend fling.

One unguarded moment. A moral hiccup. It felt like a cruel act of karma. *Karma.* That's what her colleagues attributed their misfortunes to.

Ashley knew that all the blame shifting in the world couldn't negate the fact that there was a life growing inside her. How was she going to break the news to Christopher? Her mind raced, imagining various gut-knotting reactions. Surely he would embrace the idea of beginning a family, even if earlier than expected. Then again, there was his best friend, Tyler, who'd convinced *his* girlfriend to terminate their unplanned pregnancy.

The grueling midnight conversation with Christopher was heart-wrenching. During the next few weeks, Ashley tried to sort through feelings of rejection and abandonment after Christopher broke up with her. She also had to sort through her "options," as her doctor had called them. Should she abort this child? Or should she bite the bullet, hope for the best, and keep her baby?

Six months later, Mckayla was born, and life never looked more beautiful.

The journey to becoming brave usually lands us at the intersection of indecision and determination. It takes courage to make something good out of a mess. The choices we make after we've made a mess of things will determine whether our mistakes lead to bigger messes or to redemptive grace. I believe you are courageous enough to grab grace around the neck and hold on tight. Be strong enough to release what is hurtful and embrace what is challenging. Only then will you rise up and discover your brave heart.

It's *in there.* You were wired for it.

Does God care if we are brave? Disney obviously does. From Mulan to Merida, the aim of Disney's marketing department is selling the notion that a *real* princess would rather wield a weapon than wait on a prince. But what if it was God who created the original warrior princess, and Disney just cashed in on God's design?

The journey to becoming brave usually lands us at the intersection of indecision and determination.

Let's walk back to the garden of Eden and steal a look at the original script:

> Then the LORD God said, "It is not good for the man to be alone. I will make a helper who is right for him." (Genesis 2:18)

In act 1, God placed Adam in a garden and gave him authority to develop the territory into a beautiful paradise. After careful examination God decided a second act was needed. He would create a helper for Adam. A female helper.

The word *helper* comes from the Hebrew word *ezer,* which is a combination of two root words, one meaning "to be strong, brave" and the other meaning "to rescue, save."[1] God first used this word to describe woman, then fourteen times to describe *Himself,* the *ezer* helping His people fight their enemies. Reread those last few sentences. Can you feel the force behind the four-letter word *ezer*? Women of all ages, listen carefully. We were not a postscript at the end of creation.

18

We are not leftover scrap material from a bad trial run. In fact, just the opposite. God chose certain of His own traits— His strength, His bravery, His protectiveness—along with attributes from His finest creation—man—and with perfect precision melded the two together to compose a female, a *brave savior.* Perhaps that explains our natural compulsion to reach for those sinking in a pit of guilt, to rescue the emotionally crushed, to seek out the lonely, love unconditionally, and forgive the undeserving. We were not wired weak. We were born brave.

How society looks at and often labels the sisterhood has more impact on our image than we've imagined. Without jumping off a psychological cliff, let me entertain you with an interesting study on culture classification: In Judaism, names are believed to be the channel by which life reaches you from above. In fact, the Kabbalists believe that when you name a child, you experience a minor prophecy.[2] They also believe the destiny of the child is wrapped up in the combination of Hebrew letters that makes up the child's name. If that assumption is true, then God's name for our female tribe, Ezer, makes our destiny fabulously fierce.

Now it makes sense. The world is after what makes us most like God. By divine design we are wired to be redeemers and warriors. In one tiny word God spelled out the destiny of our gender: *Brave. Strong. Rescuer. Savior.* Any lesser labeling of women is a lie. Marketing firms invest billions in infomercials, billboards, hyperlink ads, pornography, weight-loss shams, money scams, and all manner of propaganda to manipulate the truth and leave us feeling flawed or "less than." And most demeaning of all, they use our fellow sisters as poster girls in their campaign. If we are not mindful of these tactics, those lies will become liabilities that will drag us down and away from our destinies.

Am I a feminist? No. I am an *ezer*.

⌒

Being an *ezer* isn't always easy.

The sight of a ferocious dog charging your husband is frightening. The sound of his leg snapping in six pieces is unforgettable. After being away for twelve days, there was nothing I wanted more than a few relaxing moments with the man I love. One block from our home, our Friday night date turned tragic.

I can still pull up the memory as if it happened yesterday. The sound of bone crunching against pavement still roars in my ears. I'd like to say I was spiritually prepared for that moment. But I wasn't. I suppose we'd all like to believe the accumulation of hours in the prayer chair would have us ready to handle whatever injustice life hurls our way. Not always.

In slow motion my mind replays the scene. Dogs barking, a drone circling, a golf cart on the sidewalk, ducks splashing in the lake, the smell of sweat, and the grinding of gears just before the near-fatal crash.

A crowd gathered at the site, attempting to piece together what had just happened. A large dog had crashed into the front of my husband's bike. I watched as his body lifted into the air and then collided with the pavement. My vision blurred and my mind tried not to race ahead. *Keep it together. Don't panic. Pick him up. Find a ride; you can get him to the hospital quicker than the ambulance can get to you.*

The world is after what
makes us most like
God. By divine design
we are wired to be
redeemers and warriors.

Pulling into the closest ER, I felt confident someone could help us.

"Sorry, ma'am. We don't have a trauma surgeon qualified to assist you."

What? How can they not have a trauma surgeon on call? I was angry and fragile all at the same time. The nurse went on to tell me about another emergency center ten miles down the freeway. Guess what? They didn't have a surgeon who could help us either. How could hospitals send a critically injured man home because they can't figure out how to help him? Not once but twice?

This agony went on for more than three weeks. We would visit two hospitals, three surgeons, and a trauma unit before finally finding a specialist who would agree to perform the operation my husband needed. During that time a Harvard-alum specialist gave us grim news: "I'm not saying there isn't *someone* who can help you, but there is nothing *I* can do to help you."

Another surgeon, in another town: "I'm sorry; I can't help you. If the surgery doesn't go well, you may never walk again, and there is a chance you could lose your leg."

Lose . . . your . . . leg.

Those three words slipped out of the surgeon's mouth in slow motion. My husband looked pale and fainted against the wall. Our normal had just been stolen.

It only takes a slight tragic turn to remind us how fragile life is. In the six months of my husband's physical recovery, we experienced a renewed sensitivity to people fighting for day-to-day courage. The morning following my husband's accident, I was scheduled to speak at a women's conference across town.

Sleep-deprived and shell-shocked, I walked onto the stage and spoke about healing and the power of divine intervention.

Did I have any assurance my husband would walk again or not lose his leg? No, but the longer I spoke, the more my *ezer* showed up on that stage. Before our session ended, I prayed with many women who needed to reclaim their courage. They weren't timid prayers that tumbled off my lips; they were bold prayers charged with expectation. I prayed over families as if they were *my* family. I spoke over their dreams with confidence those dreams would change history. And, aware that hell's mission is to destroy our families' destinies, I prayed with a fervency that drove fear out of the room. This wasn't the first attack on my own family, by the way; this was the fifth tragedy in thirty days. I'm not talking about head colds; I am referring to satanic attacks designed to hinder our appointment with divine destiny.

I don't know if you have ever felt like a moving target that hell longs to take out, but a quiet inner voice tells me you have. While the details of your story may be different from mine, the strategy to dismantle your faith and courage is the same. That statement isn't meant to alarm you but to alert you. My goal is to empower you to take on and defeat the foe that threatens to wear you down.

God didn't give you a brave heart and a timid tongue. No, He paired your brave heart with a tongue that has creative power. What we say is far more impactful than we think. Our words are arrows that can launch a counterassault against our enemy. I've learned that the secret to hitting your enemy is hitting your knees and opening your mouth—in prayer.

Every great story has an intriguing backdrop. That is true of all sixty-six books of the Bible. It's my nature to study the backstory of the characters before trying to put the story line into context. This week, as I started studying the first book of Samuel, I was intrigued that the author didn't begin the historical account of the kings of Israel with a war but with a birth. As I peeled back a few layers, I discovered a man vulnerable enough to put his personal drama out in the open. In fact, his story reads like sound bites from a TMZ episode or headlines on a tabloid: "Polygamist Wives Brawl" or "Priest Confronts Suspected Drunk Woman at Mass."

Am I trying to be cute with Scripture? No. It would just do most of us good to pause and place biblical history in modern-day vernacular. Follow along as we read a modern translation of these verses:

> But [Peninnah] taunted [Hannah], . . . *never letting her forget* that God had not given her children. This went on year after year. *Every time* she went to the sanctuary of God she could expect to be taunted. . . .
>
> It so happened that as [Hannah] *continued in prayer* before God, Eli [the priest] was watching her closely. Hannah was praying in her heart, silently. Her lips moved, but no sound was heard. Eli jumped to the conclusion that she was drunk. He approached her and said, "You're drunk! How long do you plan to keep this up? Sober up, woman!"
>
> Hannah said, "Oh no, sir—please! . . . I haven't been drinking. Not a drop of wine or beer. The only thing I've been pouring out is my heart, pouring it out to God. (1 Samuel 1:6–7, 12–15 THE MESSAGE, emphasis added)

What's worse than morning sickness? Crying yourself to sleep because fertility specialists have given you less than 1 percent chance of conceiving a child. *Infertility.* The word sets off alarm bells in the head of any woman wanting a child. *No, it's not him . . . it's you.* And the only sounds more deafening are the taunts of an adversary or an accusation from a man of God.

Honestly, I don't know how Hannah handled herself with such dignity. Given the same situation, I bet most of us would put on a giant emotional production, including a three-ring act showcasing the shallowest part of our faith. Maybe that was you just this past week. Don't feel judged. I've spent more years conducting emotional circuses than I care to remember. What set me free from the emotional triggers that robbed my courage and stole my dignity? One powerful little word: *prayer.*

When I mention prayer, I am not referencing the soft words of someone unsure her appeal will make it past the bedroom ceiling. I'm referring to courageous words that roar out of one's spirit. No, they don't have to be loud, but they do have to be convincing.

Rocking back and forth, Hannah wept. As her tears hit the cold marble floor, her lips quivered out prayers with no sound. Hannah prayed with such fervor and conviction that the priest asked her to dial it down. To regain her composure. To show some dignity. Hannah wasn't concerned with any show of counterfeit dignity. She was concerned with storming heaven's gates.

It has come to my attention that the more reckless our prayers become, the more ruthless people are in their reactions. Small, timid prayers don't agitate others. But try praying an impractical prayer in a public place. That's sure to shift some things around. You may even have some inner-circle friends squirming when you pray. Pray anyway. Become so comfortable with the uncomfortable that your faith moves the faithless out of your way.

I've always believed that prayer rewards the private requests of our hearts. Over time, I've also discovered it locks shut the mouths of our critics. The irony of Hannah's story is that Eli the priest mocked the intercession of the woman carrying the very child whom God had appointed to serve him. How our human interaction must make God laugh. The truth is, a priest may have accused Hannah, but the High Priest exonerated her. The more she prayed, the more God moved. In fact, He transformed her story from a tacky tabloid tale to a headline story in biblical history. When a woman knows how to touch God with her prayers, anything and everything is possible. Yet far too often our prayers go unanswered because we care too much about what others think and too little about what God longs to do.

I can sit in a restaurant for less than ten minutes and ascertain the level of intimacy between couples. Those with any emotional distance between them avoid eye contact. But for-lifers lean in, look each other in the eyes, listen, and talk to each other without flinching. Similarly, I can determine how intimate a woman is with God by how she prays. Over the decades, I have listened to thousands of women pray. In fact, I often ask women to pray before a lunch or a meeting. It's not their conversation with me that clues me in on what I want to know; it's that prayer offered before our conversation that gives me the inside track on whether the woman knows God, or only knows *about* God. A woman who really knows her God, whatever the volume of her voice, prays bold, audacious, *messy* prayers. Not tentative, faltering, excuse-me-for-bothering-you prayers, but prayers that cut through all the pretense—and cut to the chase. God is looking to do awe-inspiring things through this generation of women. Grander things than any of us dare imagine. But we will never live up to our potential as *ezers* until we dispense with timid prayers. Timid prayers do nothing to move us forward; if anything, they highlight our deeply rooted fears and keep us treading in the shallow end of living. Now is not the time to draw back in fear. It is time for the daughters of destiny to rise up and pray risky prayers that force hell to tremble. It's what we were made for.

We cannot trust our culture to define the role of women in these final hours of history. God alone holds that classified envelope. If we are passionate about holding in our hands what God longs to give us, we must first know what's in His heart. That happens best in a prayer closet. The journey to rising up and changing our world doesn't begin by walking down the cushy road of modernism. It begins by rediscovering the ancient path of prayer—bold, audacious prayer.

> It is time for the daughters of destiny to rise up and pray risky prayers that force hell to tremble.

Don't wait until the end of this book to begin your prayer odyssey. If you have any aspirations of breaking out of survival mode, reigniting your passion for living, and daring to dream wild and live fear-free, then I want you to drop to your knees—right now. If prayer is new for you or you've never really developed a habit of it, then this is the day for you to step outside your comfort zone. It's time you were liberated from everything that has brought you down and kept you down thus far. Find somewhere to pray. A closet. A corner. A chapel. Whatever makes you feel at home with your heavenly Father. Tuck a journal under your arm and take it with you. Scribble down your thoughts. Paint a fresh plan for your life. Sketch your name beside that next big dream. Your journal will be more than a diary detailing your journey. It will be an heirloom of your history and a testament to your *bravery*.

The bravery you were wired with.

Further Reflection

1. When was the last time you backed away from a situation because it made you feel insecure? How could you have responded more bravely?

2. What negative thoughts do you find yourself meditating on most often? Have you always entertained these thoughts, or did they develop over time? If the latter, at what point in your life did these thoughts begin to form? What events led to their formation?

3. Read Genesis 2:18. Why did God create woman? Now review the origin of the word *ezer* from this chapter. What characteristics mark an *ezer*? Do you possess those qualities? (Hint: You were *created* with them.)

4. Take a moment to evaluate your interactions with God. Do you tend to pray halting, hesitant prayers, or do you "approach God's throne of grace with confidence" (Hebrews 4:16 NIV)? What would you consider a "messy" prayer?

chapter
THREE

CHANGING YOUR
TRAJECTORY

Neatly filed away in the ancient book of Numbers is a story line that rewards those who manage to peel open their eyelids long enough to read the laundry list of who begat whom. In the twenty-seventh chapter of this book are six powerful words that forever changed the trajectory of our gender: *"The daughters of Zelophehad showed up"* (Numbers 27:1 THE MESSAGE, emphasis added).

Chapter 26 sets the stage . . .

Dust. Sweat. Body odor. A meeting for men, about *men things*. The five daughters of Zelophehad stood gawking at the edge of the testosterone-filled crowd gathered on the plains of Moab. Their leader, Moses; Eliezer, the priest; and the council of leaders stood together at the entrance of the Tent of Meeting. Moses had just taken a census—of the men. God wanted to build an army, He'd said, so Moses had numbered all the males. Fathers. And sons. There wasn't another female in sight.

What were they thinking? There wasn't a chance their request would be granted. Still, these sisters had come.

The sisters had heard the news. After Moses had counted all the men, he'd separated them by clan. It was time to distribute the land among the *men* and their *sons.* God Himself had instructed Moses to divide up the land based on clan size: the smaller the clan, the smaller the inheritance. The sisters had also heard names spoken—all men's. No surprise there. Everyone knew it was the men who inherited property. Land was passed from a father to his sons to their sons, and so on.

But *they* weren't sons—and they surely weren't soldiers. They were their dead father's only children—and they were women.

But they were women on a mission.

Clustered together, the sisters moved toward the tent like a swarm of bees, the eldest sister, Mahlah, at the lead. The men obviously resented their presence. Mahlah could feel their hostile glares as she bumped elbows and politely excused herself. But their entire future depended on this day and the verdict that would be handed down.

At last they reached Moses. His piercing gaze turned to them.

The sisters' faces went pale. Their lips trembled as their leader made eye contact with each of them. When his eyes met the eldest sister's, she wanted to shrink from his gaze . . . but it was now or never. She summoned up her bravery and stepped forward.

"Our father died in the wilderness," she began. "But *he* wasn't part of Korah's rebellion."

Oh no. She was rambling. Why had she even brought up

that rebellion? *Get to the point, Mahlah!* she chided herself. She took a deep breath . . . and then just blurted it out. "Well, we don't have any brothers. Our father only had daughters." She twirled her finger in a motion that took in herself and her four younger sisters. "This is it." Then jutting out her chin defiantly, she demanded, "But why should our father's name die out just because he had no *sons? We* want an inheritance too!"

Unprecedented! Mahlah could hear the gasps behind her. Never had a woman dared to make such a demand. But she'd come this far. She *would* see it through. Boldly she insisted, "Give us some land, *just like everybody else.*"

Silence. You could have heard a pin drop. The crowd held their breath.

Moses turned to the priest and the council, and they huddled. Then Moses disappeared into the Tent of Meeting—to bring their case before God.

After what seemed like hours, Moses stepped out of the tent and motioned for the crowd to hear God's ruling: "Zelophehad's daughters are right. Give them land . . . Give them their father's inheritance" (Numbers 27:6–7 THE MESSAGE).

Several thousand men let out a collective breath. Women would now be landowners. Five sisters and one daring question had changed the trajectory for women for all time.

The turning point in the history of women's rights can be traced back to five audacious sisters who dared to challenge a culture that had been oblivious to their gender's needs. Rereading their story makes me question: Up to that point, had men simply withheld property from women and the women were just *never brave enough* to ask for their inheritance?

I'm going to take a risk and wade out into an area that may have us swimming for the shallow end before we are through.

For generations our gender has been taught that men are our primary oppressors. I admit, in many cultures women are subjugated. But with that acknowledgment I must also concede that our timidity and complacency are not *entirely* the fault of men. Before we cry, "Victim!" and excuse away our withering dreams, we must ask if we have voraciously fought to shift the trajectory of our culture. Have we seized every opportunity within reach, and have we been as committed to holding open doors for each other as we have for ourselves?

Let's be plain. Zelophehad's daughters faced the complex issue of not having a man around to represent their cause or stand against injustice. No father. No brother. No husband. I am all too familiar with the insecurities that arise when there isn't a man around. I grew up without a father. I wasn't raised with the assurance that if I were to slip, I would have a safe place to fall. There was no one to call when money ran thin or hysteria set in. My foundation of fatherhood wasn't just cracked; it was nonexistent.

It's hard to wrap your mind around the concept of *inheritance* when there has been no *heritage*. It took decades for me to realize that my lack of human heritage didn't cancel my entitlement to a superior spiritual inheritance. Maybe this isn't a huge revelation to you, but it was life altering for me. When I discovered God's inheritance bypassed my bloodline, that single revelation gave me confidence to ask for the improbable and reach for the impossible. My faith took a hard right, and for the first time I began to experience what I had previously only imagined.

While your story may be quite different from Mahlah's or mine, I can guarantee that somewhere along your journey, the enemy of your destiny has tried to sell you the lie that, like the sisters in our Bible story, you are unworthy of God's promises. Don't slip-slide into deception. There is nothing God enjoys more than answering the requests of His daughters. But it is our responsibility to arise and ask for our inheritance.

Think on this: Every generation is defined by the questions they ask or refuse to ask. What would you ask for if you knew the answer to your request was going to be *yes*? Most of us don't receive the miracles we crave because voices of doubt make us feel unqualified for supernatural intervention. We bury our dreams beneath excuses and insecurities. We stop dreaming the moment it gets daring. What would happen if, like Zelophehad's daughters, we became hungry enough to demand our inheritance? What if we were daring enough to ask for something we haven't seen with our eyes, only our spirits?

My cell phone buzzed. It was late. On the other end of the call was my friend Rosie. She asked if I had time to talk. Having just wrapped up back-to-back speaking engagements, I didn't have energy for a long-winded conversation and started to say no. But the persistent tone of Rosie's voice let me know this was borderline urgent. She asked if I would join her on a three-way call with a lady named Jada. Hesitantly, I agreed, and Jada began to unravel her story.

Don't stop dreaming

the moment it

gets daring.

A single mom of boys, Jada lived in a less-than-desirable neighborhood just south of Detroit. For the last year, her prayer life had centered on asking God to provide a way for her boys to live in a safer neighborhood where they could attend charter schools. Outside of a miracle, the move seemed impossible. But Jada had continued to pray. The more she prayed, the more specific her prayers became. She went from asking God to do something believable to trusting God for a taste of the supernatural. The safe, comfortable prayers she'd once prayed shifted to radical if not risky appeals to heaven.

One Saturday afternoon Jada decided to drive around the border of her city and pray. Hours passed as Jada's tiny compact wagon circled the perimeter. Southwest on Interstate 75, north on 96, back east on 94. Round and round she went. With each lap she surrendered her doubts; with each loop she surrounded her promise. The farther she drove, the stronger her prayers became. These were not frivolous shots in the dark; they were arrows of faith launched from Earth, aiming to pierce the ceiling of heaven.

Now, driving in circles is not how most people choose to pray. But I've seen enough miracles to know sometimes the greatest ones aren't launched from a prayer chair but behind a high chair. Sometimes they're launched from behind the wheel. God cares less about where we pray and more about how we pray. And heaven isn't moved by our posture; it's shaken by our passion.

After three hours of circling the city, Jada's car and prayer vigil made an abrupt turn. Uncertain of her location, she pulled over at a small cul-de-sac and looked around. To the right was a small patch of woods; to the left was a beautiful home with a small sign in the window that read For Sale by Owner. Jada felt curiously drawn to the house, so she got out of her car, walked up the drive, and peered into the window. The front door opened, and a tall elderly man asked if she would like to see the home. Caught off guard, she stammered out an apology and turned to leave. The man asked again if she would like to see the house. Feeling rather foolish, Jada said yes.

One glass of tea, then two, and a quick tour of the home turned into hours of conversation as Jada, Joe, and his wife, Marg, babbled on like lifelong friends. For the engrossed trio, time slipped by even after the hours passed.

After a warm goodbye Jada made her way to the door. As she turned to leave, Joe looked at Marg and said, "I think the woman we've been waiting on has finally arrived."

"Excuse me?" Jada said, confused.

Joe went on to explain. He and Marg had purchased a new home across town but agreed not to move until they found the person to whom they were to *give* their current home. They had spent months praying, waiting on the right person to arrive and take possession of the small estate. It was clear to both that Jada was the one God had in mind when He gave them a vision of blessing someone with their home.

True to that vision, two months later, the title was transferred to Jada, and her sons now live in a debt-free home and attend charter schools.

That is the thing I have come to appreciate about miracle moments: No one can predict them; no one can control them. What appears accidental, God has arranged.

Can I state the obvious? Radical prayers produce irrational results. Maybe you're not digging your heels in for a home, but I am confident there is something written on the wish list of your heart. Be assured that God loves answering prayers of faith, performing the impossible, and fulfilling His daughters' secret dreams. That is the Father's heart, to astonish His daughters with His goodness.

Prayer is a verbal reflection of our confidence in God. It is an opportunity to acknowledge that our Father is in charge of every situation, great and small. By articulating our faith and affection, we draw God's goodness into the daily grind. Whatever storm you are encountering, remember to make time for small prayer breaks. Embrace quiet, reflective moments. Unlock the windows of heaven with your words of faith and adoration.

God loves answering prayers of faith, performing the impossible, and fulfilling His daughters' secret dreams.

While I have no idea what is on your private wish list, I am convinced that you are one bold request, one prayer drive, one worship-filled night away from encountering the miraculous. Even now I sense that God longs to place within our reach things previous generations of women have been denied. You see, there is far more to our story than what our culture would have us believe. Culture points to a woman standing in a garden and violating God's command. It ignores God promise that the Savior of humanity would come through that fallen woman's legacy. That's what shame does best: it focuses on our failures in order to dilute our faith.

Several weeks ago, I visited the home of a very wealthy

woman. Tall, thin, curved in all the right places, she was the envy of most women—until she pulled the covers off her broken heart. I sat patiently, hour after hour, listening to her bemoan how unhappy and unfulfilled she was. At the end of the conversation, it was crystal clear: shame had squeezed the life out of her. And she's not the only one.

Just yesterday I received a text from a friend who was convinced she should give up teaching her women's group at church. The enemy kept reminding her of wrongs she had committed . . . *twenty years ago*. It took hours of convincing to strip away the layers of built-up shame. There is still much work to do in patching up her self-confidence.

Then this morning, as I was leaving for the airport, I received six frantic text messages from a woman I've known for more than a decade. As I scanned her texts, I experienced an unwelcome déjà vu. Yep. I could almost quote her line for line. Shame had come to call. I wanted to throw the phone, not at her but at the enemy who has blinded her.

How many times do we fall on the very sword that has just tried to decapitate us? If the enemy can't succeed at destroying us himself, then he'll make sure we do it *for* him. Seriously. We can't deny the truth. We are all guilty of emotional self-mutilation. It happens the moment we quit discounting the enemy's lies and start believing them.

Let's pause and reason this out. What if Eve had believed that a bite of fruit would disqualify her forever from redemption? I'm sure the enemy whispered such scandalous lies. He is diligent in attempting to sabotage our future with poisonous arrows of anxiety and shame. But it's one thing to hear the words of the accuser; it's another to believe them.

Now is not the time to wrap ourselves in sheets of shame. Only defeated warriors walk around with their heads buried in shame. We have pled guilty far too long. It's time we stop walking to the witness stand and testifying against ourselves. We are too strong for that. Shame will never let you move forward. It will only hold you back from God's greater purpose. So, rise up and courageously stare your accuser in the face. That's one of the *bravest* things you'll ever do.

Let me get this out of the way up front: I am in no way endorsing the television series I am about to reference. In full disclosure, I only needed to check out the pilot episode of *Breaking Bad* to decide its content landed far outside my comfort zone. But I admit the episode I viewed had me squirming on the edge of my favorite ottoman. For days I thought about the main character, Walter White, a high school chemistry teacher recently diagnosed with inoperable lung cancer. Until that diagnosis, Walter was a straitlaced loner working a job beneath his qualifications. When he learns he has just months to live, he is forced to reexamine his life. How will he spend the days he has left? How will he secure his family's future? To everyone's shock, Walter changes trajectories and decides to manufacture and sell meth to provide for his family after his death.

Without question the story line is dark and depraved. My point in sharing the plot is this: How often do *we* plod through life, accepting things as they come without considering that our days may be fewer than we think? It breaks my heart to think of women who silently crave more out of life but will never fully awaken to their dreams until their time has come to an end.

What would you fight for if your days were numbered? What dream would you resurrect if you weren't stuck in the trenches of monotony and boredom? If you knew time was slipping away, what would you battle to get back? What injustice would you begin to make right? The truth is, our time *is* limited.

I feel there is a holy dissatisfaction God is using to awaken His chosen women. Tucked away in the book of the prophet Isaiah is this compelling plea:

> Awake, awake, put on strength,
> O arm of the LORD;
> awake, as in days of old,
> the generations of long ago.
>
> (Isaiah 51:9 ESV)

This isn't just a prophetic charge for the late eighth century; this is an appeal to God for *this* generation as well. We are living in a society that is witnessing an increase in human trafficking, violence, corporate discrimination against women, hunger, poverty, political instability, economic uncertainty, and social unrest. Up to now, many would rather look the other way than deal with the issues at hand. We've buried our heads in busy schedules, focusing on the familiar and making giants out of the unimportant.

But I believe God has heard Isaiah's cry and is awakening His daughters from their drowsy daydreams. He is calling us to rise up and make room for each other. I know it won't be easy. Well-won victories come with an expensive price tag. Uniting women in a culture that pits us against each other is a tall order.

But if we are going to develop into warriors that make a difference, we must begin living life on God's terms. For many of us, that means "breaking bad." We'll have to pray harder, look deeper, love more. For all of us, it means we will have to be *brave*.

My Walter White wake-up call came years ago—long before *Breaking Bad*—when God asked me to withdraw a large sum of money from my savings account and give it to a woman who was fighting a cause greater than my own. I had dreams. But she was actually living hers.

I was attending a conference, seated seven rows from the front, when I felt God nudge me to take a leap of faith and make a donation that defied my current level of generosity.

God, are You serious?

Clearly, I was mistaken. After all, the money God was prompting me to give wasn't from my personal spending account; it was from my vision account. For more than a year, I had stashed every dollar I could save to purchase new television equipment. I had already selected which stations our programs would air on, and pictures of those networks were securely bound in my dream book. The money I had tucked away was almost enough to slide my dream from the vision column to the reality column.

> Uniting women in a culture that pits us against each other is a tall order.

Silently, I wrestled. To obey God would push the fulfillment of my dreams far down the line. Surely the way to achieve my dream wasn't to sacrifice my dream. That's not how God does things . . . right?

Sitting slump-shouldered in my chair, I tried to recall stories where God rewarded illogical obedience. Even though I knew hundreds of examples, in that moment I couldn't imagine a single scenario that didn't make that leap of faith look anything less than fatal. Not one.

Sometimes there is nothing glamorous about obeying God. In fact, it can get quite messy.

The night God asked me to give away my *dream fund*, my initial instinct was to say no. *Why should I say yes?* I reasoned. *What's in it for me?* I couldn't think of any way God could bring anything good out of giving up my dream.

Have you ever felt that way after God had invited you to live your faith out loud and make a bold move that wasn't what you signed up for? Then don't feel bad. You're not the only one. Moses felt that way, too, and even argued with God—frequently. Jonah didn't just resist his assignment; he dropped it like a hot stone and ran the opposite direction. Maybe you didn't argue or resist, but like Sarah, you laughed out loud. Or maybe, like Peter, you just sank (Exodus 4:1–17; Jonah 1; Genesis 18:1–15; Matthew 14:22–32). People of faith don't always start out fearless; sometimes the worrier has to evolve into a warrior.

Let me bring this story full circle. The night of the conference, with fear and faith meshed together, I wrote out a check and placed it in the guest speaker's hand. I hate to leave you on an anticlimactic note, but there was no divine applause, and no angels sang.

But I'm certain God winked.

Fast-forward six months. I had just wrapped up the final service of a conference in Los Angeles and was on my way out. A guest pastor greeted me.

"I enjoyed your message," he said.

"Thank you," I replied.

"Is there a way I can hear more of your messages?" he continued. "Do you have a television program on satellite or cable?"

Feeling foolish, I answered, "To be honest, our programs haven't aired on the West Coast yet."

"Why not?"

Deep sigh. How could I explain placing our television programs on hold because I had given my dream fund to a guest speaker? I rambled off excuses and briefly shared our team's dream of someday having a program in the area. With just minutes to get to the airport, my assistant motioned that it was time to go. I politely thanked the pastor again and turned to leave. But before I could get away, the pastor handed me his card and said, "Our church recently purchased five new television cameras. Truthfully, we only need four. Have your staff contact my office and we will ship one of the cameras to you next week."

> People of faith don't always start out fearless; sometimes the worrier has to evolve into a warrior.

And there you have it: a full-circle miracle moment. Unexpected. Unanticipated. But right on schedule.

The greatest stories of your life will likely begin with the four-letter word *r-i-s-k*. It takes courage to push aside your fears and move forward with your instincts. And it requires a great deal of faith to set free those things that you would rather control and instead do what God says to do.

But this is your appointed time.

God is perfectly positioning you right where He needs you. Don't be afraid to follow His lead. It will change your trajectory.

FOR

Further Reflection

1. Read Numbers 27:1–11. How did the actions of the five sisters in that story change history? What decisive action could *you* take that might change your story—and maybe history itself—if only you were brave enough?

2. What would you ask for if you knew the answer to your request was going to be yes? (Think outside the box.) What is keeping you from trusting God with those desires—and asking for them? Note: James 4:2 says, "Ye have not, because ye ask not" (KJV).

3. What lies does the enemy tell you over and over? Have you believed them? What have these lies kept you from attempting? Are you ready to shake them off for good and move forward?

4. Has God ever asked you to give up a dream of your own to enable someone else's dream? Did you obey? If so, what was the outcome? If you didn't obey, is it too late to say yes to God and step out in faith?

chapter
FOUR

THE FLASHING
BLADE

On board an Air Canada flight from Montreal, I snuggled down in my seat and scanned the in-flight movie options. Looking for something more along the lines of adventure than drama, I went for the new release of *Wonder Woman*.[1] Nearing $800 million in worldwide sales, this story was certain to be told in epic fashion. I wasn't disappointed.

In case you're not familiar with the cinematic version of *Wonder Woman*, let me run you through the plot:

The screenplay opens along the picturesque shores of Themyscira, home to Diana, the youngest of the Amazon women and the daughter of the god Zeus. Diana lives an idyllic existence until army pilot Steve Trevor crashes his plane off the island shore. Through Steve she learns that the outside world is engulfed in a war threatening to destroy civilization. After hearing horror stories of human suffering, Diana decides to leave her homeland and use her powers to put an end to the bloodshed. Convinced she was created to save the world, she sets out on a journey to stop the war.

I know this story line may sound familiar, perhaps like a laundry list of other superhero tales spun out over the decades. Without getting into an argument, I must object to throwing this tale in with other skinny-ended story lines with similar plots. This movie has merit. In fact, its plot reflects more about our gender than any soft romance script.

You are probably wondering, in a world overrun by aggression, wars, and violence, why take time to focus on a film filled with the same themes? I reference this movie because it mirrors the heartbeat of every woman-warrior whose longstanding desire is to fight for something greater than herself. It is the story line of women who've grown tired of skipping through life without grabbing their destinies by the tail. This plot takes into account those confident women who are ready to be architects of their own destinies.

Can I be real? Society has done our gender no favors when it comes to helping us embrace our femininity. In fact, there is a full-out feminist campaign to make women *brash* but not *brave*. Don't be easily deceived. You can be both feminine and fierce. Those words are not antithetical. One doesn't cancel the other out. If anything, they are a lethal combination, highlighting God's original design to use our feminine strength for His glory. We were created to transform hate into love, hostility into human kindness, and to discover hope in the midst of horror.

Whether we realize it or not, like Diana, we are a part of an epic battle. The battle is not simply a part of our destiny. The battle *is* our destiny. So embed this truth in your heart: you were created to be a brave, unapologetic warrior.

We have already discussed this concept in our study of the word *ezer*, and we will take a deeper look at this revelation again. By the time you close this book, Diana will not be the only "Wonder Woman" who evolves and takes her place in the hall of heroines. I believe you, too, will arise and embrace the lofty calling of being a brave warrior.

As my plane floated along at thirty thousand feet, I studied the evolution of Diana. I paid close attention to those transfor-

You can be both feminine and fierce. One doesn't cancel the other out.

mational moments that would mold her into a world changer. Although I don't have time to discuss all the strong metaphors in the script, I do want to share the ones related to your destiny.

My favorite scene of the film is when Steve brings Diana to the edge of the battle and tells her there is no way to win the war. Darkness is stronger than light, he explains. And human suffering, hate, and destruction are simply a part of life.

Diana, seeing the carnage of war and people dying all around her, yells at Steve, "So . . . what? So we do nothing?"

"No, *we are* doing something!" Steve argues. "We are! We just . . . we can't save everyone in this war. This is not what we came here to do."

"No," agrees Diana. "But it's what *I'm* going to do."

Diana has perhaps the greatest moral clarity of any superhero in cinematic history. She deftly sweeps aside others' attempts to dismiss her mission: *saving those who cannot defend themselves.* That's what heroes do. That's what *ezers* do. That's what we all should do, and we should ignore every voice that diminishes that divine purpose.

Now is not the time to be casual and comfortable. Each of us has a heavenly mission to carry out. And that assignment is far too great to be compromised by the notion that the battle is too big for us. We must believe instead that the battle can be *won*. The strongholds *can* be conquered. We were created to save those around us, to alleviate suffering, and to put an end to injustice.

Just like Wonder Woman.

At the beginning of the screenplay, Diana discovers the Flashing Blade, a mythical sword possessing the power to destroy darkness. When she learns of the millions dying in the war to end all wars, she removes the Flashing Blade from its resting place and journeys to the front line of the battle.

The Flashing Blade had been hidden away for centuries. In time, it would be used to fight Ares, the god of darkness. But in the meantime, it had been set aside, reserved for the brave daughter created for that battle.

Did you catch the parallel? God has a Flashing Blade reserved for each of His daughters. A sharp, double-edged blade that when held in the hands of the brave, drives back the darkness. Our blade is God's Word. His truths are inscribed on our swords. As long as our swords remain strapped to our sides, we are dangerous to the enemy. Without them, we remain defenseless.

As your sister and friend, I beg you not to ever drop your guard and let the enemy catch you without your "sword," especially when you are on the battlefield, deep in enemy territory.

At one point during the film, Diana walks through the fashion district of London and a lady says to her, "I'm sorry, ma'am, but *the sword doesn't go with the outfit.*"

When I heard that line, I almost jumped out of my seat. I wanted to yell back, "What do you mean, the sword doesn't go with her outfit? The sword goes with every outfit."

And that's when I realized: those who do not know the power of the sword will always try to strip you of yours. But the Word of God is never inappropriate, so keep your hand securely wrapped around the hilt of your sword.

Stay with me on this journey as I hook on one last metaphor.

In a mesmerizing moment near the end of the movie, Diana attends a gala with the Flashing Blade securely woven into the back of her evening gown. As she dances across the marble floor, the light hits the hilt of the sword and it shimmers like a diamond. Diana understands that a sword isn't just for the battlefield but also for the ballroom. And she's right. Enemies are everywhere, even in the most pleasant of places. Make sure your sword is securely sewn into the fabric of whatever season of life you are in.

As the movie fades, one thing is made certain—Diana isn't a hero because she carries a sword but because she carries hope. In our efforts to set society's injustices aright, may we never lose sight of our hope. We can change the world, one courageous act at a time.

Sifting through a stack of papers one day, I found these words scribbled along the edge of one sheet:

Villages in Israel were deserted—deserted
until I, Deborah, took a stand—took a stand
as a mother of Israel. (Judges 5:7 GW)

What ominous words . . .

My hand trembled slightly as I read this passage. Deborah's declaration awakened a part of my slumbering soul. *Mother of Israel.* What kind of woman describes herself this way? Sinking down into my sofa cushions, I took some time to create a visual image of Deborah. My mind filtered through a dozen or more images until I felt certain I'd sketched out what this liberator looked like: I pegged her as six foot one, with thick, dark hair and a chiseled face with a firm jawline and a rather stern-looking mouth.

Isn't that what we women do? We want a patented design on how strength should be packaged, and we are offended if it arrives in a different package.

I'm guilty of false labeling, no doubt about it. Ten years ago, I would have scrawled the words *arrogant* and *self-absorbed leader* across Deborah's résumé. It's not every day that someone takes credit for saving a village. Especially when the savior isn't packaged as a *hero* but a *heroine.* There is an unspoken, universal acceptance of men talking about their exploits, but there's backlash when women do. I'm not sure where that kind of thinking evolved from, but I am confident we could trace the roots back to a garden somewhere east of Eden. For centuries we women have been taught to *look* for deliverers rather than recognize our appointment *as* deliverers. But as daughters of the King, our roles as heroines aren't optional. They are engraved in our heritage and inscribed in our destinies.

But as daughters of the King, our roles as heroines aren't optional. They are engraved in our heritage and inscribed in our destinies.

Becoming brave and confronting the challenges of our culture aren't things we merely "consider" doing; they are royal assignments from heaven. We must get comfortable with the idea that women can be confident without being arrogant. It is possible for our gender to embrace both femininity and self-confidence.

But what if no one tells us we are designed to be deliverers? What becomes of our destinies if no one instills within us the confidence to step out of our comfort zones? Or worse, what if uncaring people trample on our dreams before we get to walk out our destinies?

Last week, while jogging through our neighborhood park, I noticed three young girls chatting while checking their iPhones. I stopped to rest on the corner bench and listened in on the conversation. They talked about who was a better dancer, about problems with their parents, about movies, and about imaginary dreams. It was the dream part that caught my attention.

One girl wanted to be a famous singer and rank top ten on iTunes. Another wished for rock-hard abs, like a celebrity. The third didn't care if she was famous *or* beautiful, she just wanted to be rich. No surprises here, girls aspiring to be successful, attractive, and accepted. Sounds just like my adult friends, with a few slight differences.

Jogging away, I began to wonder, when will these young warriors be sold the lie that their dreams are no longer achievable? Who will knock the confidence out of their souls? What heartaches will wash away their hopes of a "happily ever after"? And at what point will they trade in their swords for something less confrontational and easier to carry?

The mother-warrior part of me wanted to run back, grab those girls, and pour strength into their dreams. I felt an unexplainable need to shield them from the lies that would discredit their worth and squelch their confidence. I wanted to tell them to

never stop believing in themselves
discover their voices
live so they would never regret their choices
feel invincible when staring down an enemy
speak up against injustice
empower the broken among their peers
embrace how God made them
never let circumstances define them
embrace rejection as God's way of rerouting them to
    something better
never let people place labels on them
forgive quickly
respond slowly and carefully
live courageously
fight with honor

More than anything, I wanted to beg them to keep their swords strapped firmly to their sides. I beg you to do the same.

The call came as I was pulling out of my driveway. "Hi . . . Tracey? This is Nora, I know we have you booked as our keynote in March, but something has come up and we need to cancel."

Cancel? The word exploded like a thunderstorm inside my head. This convention had been on my calendar for more than a year. In fact, our team had already booked flights and hotel rooms to support the event.

After a long pause I forced back the tears and tried to respond in a normal-sounding voice. "Cancel or postpone?"

"Actually, we need to cancel. We've double-booked our speakers and . . ."

I don't remember the rest of the explanation because I knew whatever words were rolling off her tongue were completely untrue. There was no double booking. It was a slick political maneuver by a colleague's publicist. I knew it. They knew it. For a moment I forgot God knew it. Slouching down in the driver's seat, I felt an urge to drop the accelerator and crash headlong into the trash bin. I didn't. I couldn't. If God wasn't watching, the neighbors were. Even though I can't remember how the botched withdrawal unfolded, my heart is warmed by the memory of God arranging a better opportunity for the weekend that was canceled.

People aren't always fair. But God is always just.

If we are not vigilant in guarding our hearts, we will allow careless people to drain the life right out of our dreams. Maybe your story isn't exactly like mine, but I bet you've had a few poisoned arrows shot your way; maybe one of them even hit its intended target and you're now looking at the headstone of your most treasured dream. Sigh. I feel for you even as I carve out these words. I can sense your heartache. Oh, how I would love to have a cup of coffee with you and talk through your pain until victory comes. It would make my heart happy to watch God's favor redeem areas of your life that the enemy has ravaged. Nothing would make me feel better than to see healing invade the places you've been violated most and see restoration seam together your fractured heart. I've experienced my share of poisoned arrows.

And yet, I am reminded, with all the things people do to sabotage our potential, they are often not the true culprits but simply pawns in the hand of a much bigger enemy.

If we are going to uproot the vines that would choke our future, we must make a startling admission: often, it is not *other* people at the root of our problems; it's us. Our own unrealistic expectations derail us. We expect everyone to love us. To support us. To praise us. To validate us. And when they don't, it shakes our foundations and our confidence.

Every time I find myself looking for validation from others, I hear a voice deep within saying, "If you're longing for approval, don't look around, look up." And yet, how many times have I fallen into the pit of despair precisely because I *didn't* look up? How many times have *you*?

So now, whenever I need strength and validation, I turn to the frayed pages of my Bible, and then I am validated—by my heavenly Father:

> If you're longing for approval, don't look around, look up.

> The LORD is the portion of my inheritance and
>   my cup;
> You support my lot.
> The lines have fallen to me in pleasant places;
> Indeed, my heritage is beautiful to me.
> I will bless the LORD who has counseled me;

Indeed, my mind instructs me in the night.
I have set the LORD continually before me;
Because He is at my right hand, I will not be shaken.

(Psalm 16:5–8 NASB)

Days before hosting our annual Thrive Conference, I received an email from a precious friend. It read:

> Dear Brave Sister,
> The assignment before you isn't about what you can achieve but what God can achieve through you. Do not fear enemies, they cannot touch you. Do not be shaken by what you see. Do not collapse beneath this load, for it is not yours to carry . . .

Words of encouragement went on to fill the page, and a link to Bethel Worship's song "You Make Me Brave" was attached.[2] I pray you take time to listen to this song and let it sink down deep in your soul.

FOR

Further Reflection

1. What personal battles have others told you are impossible to win? Do you tend to listen to those people and believe them, tune them out, or challenge them and try to prove them wrong?

2. In the movie discussed in this chapter, Diana is told there is no way to win the war. But Diana is the daughter of a god, and she knows who she is. You are a child of *the* God. Do you know who *you* are? If not, can you think of any scriptures that will remind you who you are and what you can achieve? Here's one for free: "I can do all things through Christ, because he gives me strength" (Philippians 4:13).

3. Read Deborah's story in Judges 4:1–16. Then read Judges 5:7. Like Deborah, we are called to be leaders. Specifically, we are to lead the women (and the children) in our generation. Who do you know that could use your strong example? How can you help them overcome their fears, develop courage, and become brave?

4. In this chapter, we identified our sword as God's Word. How well do you know your Bible? In times of fear, sorrow, worry, and trouble, can you call up scriptures to get you through? If not, would you consider seeking out a good Bible study especially for women, or joining a Bible study group so you can arm yourself with God's truth?

chapter
FIVE

A DREAM THIEF

Our meeting was sheer happenstance. Day four of a business trip to Seattle landed me in an out-of-the-way coffee shop in the village. Lined with colorful hues and earthy fabrics, it was the perfect landing spot to try out the local fare.

Slipping off my coat, I approached the barista and ordered. "French vanilla latte with an extra shot."

"Skinny or extra whip?"

"Skinny, no whip. Make it strong."

"You got it." He smiled and winked. "Hard day?"

"Long week."

He nodded. "Then let's hope this helps."

With latte and fruit bar in hand, I made my way to a cozy spot near the fire pit.

"Forgotten and alone, somewhere far from home . . ." Whispered lyrics floated in the air. "Frightened and confused, lost and refused . . ."

Ah. There was the source of the acoustic mix. Perched on a stool was a thirtysomething young woman with ash-blonde hair.

One song. Then two. The lyrics were hauntingly deep. I tried to imagine the story behind the music and quietly prayed for an opportunity to chat. That moment came after the midday break.

"Hi. I enjoyed your set."

"Thanks. It's what I do," the singer answered with a shrug.

"Your lyrics . . . are they original?"

"Often imitated, but always original."

I could tell there was a smack of pain in that last statement. "I can relate."

"Ah, someone rip off your material too?" she asked with an empathetic smirk. Not waiting for a reply, she said, "I'm Carmen," and pulled up a chair.

Before we knew it, one hour had turned into two as we swapped stories like siblings rather than strangers.

It wasn't long before tears slipped down Carmen's cheeks. Five years earlier, her manager, Stella, had swindled away the rights to Carmen's future platinum release. Years of hard work—vanished into thin air. Royalty checks went unpaid; a nationwide tour, canceled. And it wasn't just the lyrics Stella hijacked. She crept her way into the arms of Carmen's longtime lover and record producer.

Stories like Carmen's make me shudder. Honestly, when does the need for an ego boost outweigh a decade-long loyalty? But it happens. Not occasionally. Frequently. And in a millisecond, an act of disloyalty can tear apart our confidence and silence our creativity.

Most of us have crossed paths with a Stella. She may have a different name, but she wreaks the same havoc on our hearts. Living in a culture that emphasizes self-importance guarantees you will run into those who will trample on your dreams while trying to fulfill their own ambitions. The question is not whether you will have a sideswipe or two with betrayal. The question is, will you allow those blows to cheat you out of your purpose? Will wounds from someone you considered a *safe sister* keep you from trusting someone new? How far downriver will the tide of disloyalty drag you? Will it distance you from your dreams, or will it capsize them altogether? Will you casually hand over the keys to your calling—or will you gather your courage and fight for your future? Only you know the answers to those questions.

I know one thing for sure: betrayal is the number one tactic the enemy uses to steal our courage. Don't let anyone fool you: betrayal is not passive; it's personal. Through betrayal the enemy attempts to shift our focus from what God desires to give us to what others have taken from us. Most of us aren't too intimidated to at least try to reach for our destinies, but we nearly collapse at the thought of having them stripped from us. Given the opportunity, betrayal will suffocate our passion for living. It hijacks courage. It's a dream thief. A confidence killer. A foe we all know.

> Betrayal is the number one tactic the enemy uses to steal our courage.

If the enemy cannot derail our destinies through the betrayal of others, he will work overtime to make sure we betray ourselves. Let me paint you a picture of what self-sabotage looks like.

SCENE: Jesus with His inner circle of twelve
PLACE: Caesarea Philippi
TOPIC OF CONVERSATION: Who is Jesus?

Tie up the boat. Find lodging. Prep the food. Campfire devotions. A day trip across the lake had left the crew wet and weary. As the fire crackled, the lighthearted chatter suddenly took an abrupt turn. Rising from the cypress stump, Jesus asked His disciples, "Who do people say I am?"

Huh? Confused looks washed over the disciples' faces. Trick question? Joke? Hoax? *Where is He going with this?*

Someone sitting next to Thaddeus garbled out, "Some say you are John the Baptizer; some say Elijah, Jeremiah, or one of the other prophets."

Pressing them for an answer of their own, Jesus asked, "And how about you? Who do *you* say I am?"

Silence. Not a word.

Finally, Peter answered, as if for all of them: "You are the Messiah, the Son of the living God!"

Jesus whirled about. "You are blessed, Simon son of Jonah, because flesh and blood did not reveal this to you, but my Father in heaven!" (Matthew 16:17 NET). "I also say to you that you are Peter, and upon this rock I will build My church; and the gates of Hades will not overpower it" (Matthew 16:18 NASB).

Quite an endorsement for a one-line answer. *Jesus must really be impressed*, Peter probably thought.

Now fast-forward the highlight reel . . . Scan past the Last Supper . . . Keep going . . . On past Judas's betrayal . . . Right there: the mock trial of Jesus at Caiaphas's court.

Now Peter was sitting out in the courtyard, and a servant girl came to him. "You also were with Jesus of Galilee," she said. But he denied it before them all. "I don't know what you're talking about," he said. Then he went out to the gateway, where another servant girl saw him and said to the people there, "This fellow was with Jesus of Nazareth." He denied it again, with an oath: "I don't know the man!" After a little while, those standing there went up to Peter and said, "Surely you are one of them; your accent gives you away." Then he began to call down curses, and he swore to them, "I don't know the man!" Immediately a rooster crowed. Then Peter remembered the word Jesus had spoken: "Before the rooster crows, you will disown me three times." And he went outside and wept bitterly. (Matthew 26:69–75 NIV)

I may be reading too much into these verses, but I don't think the curse words Peter chose were mild ones. Probably more like the ones fishermen used at a barroom brawl. Either way, somewhere between Caesarea Philippi and Caiaphas's court, Peter's loyalty took a hard left.

Peter loved Jesus. Then Peter betrayed Jesus, right after Judas did.

If you are like me, there's no greater feeling than thinking our actions have impressed God. There are also few things that make us snap back to reality faster than feeling that we have failed God. I'm not talking about the kind of failure that seems recoverable, but the kind that makes rebounding seem impossible. At this point you may fear that I am going to ask you to dredge up a memory of when you failed God. I won't.

I have too many to pull from my own closet. So instead, let me share with you my friend Amanda's story.

I hadn't heard from Amanda in more than a year when she called and invited me to lunch. When I arrived at the restaurant, I noticed something had changed; she was different. She hadn't lost weight, changed her hairstyle, or splurged on a new wardrobe. On the surface she remained unchanged. But the tone in her voice and the forced smile gave me a quick heads-up on what was about to unfold. It would take two appetizers, an entrée, and half of a molten chocolate cake before she loosened up enough to divulge the source of her pain.

The past year had been difficult for Amanda. Having lived the last two decades in an affluent neighborhood, supported by her doting husband, she had thrived amid the security of her rural township. Beautiful and outgoing, she was a socialite and the sweetheart of the community. That abruptly changed when her husband's company transferred them from a community of eighteen thousand to the urban outskirts of Las Vegas. That sudden jolt, coupled with the unanticipated news that she was pregnant with child number three, threw Amanda into a vortex of insecurity. Even more devastating, her mother had been diagnosed with stage 4 cancer.

Unprepared for the roller-coaster ride of change, Amanda began making poor choices that led her down a self-destructive path. Emotionally jarred and hormonally unbalanced, she found herself romantically involved with not one but two men online. When her husband, Reese, found out about her online escapades, he threatened divorce. Depressed and confused by her own behavior, Amanda retreated into isolation and was now even more disconnected from reality than before. That's what betrayal does best. It makes lonely look enticing. It tries to convince us that isolation guarantees security, protecting us from others. Let me assure you: isolation doesn't provide insulation; it just creates a bigger issue. And how can you pursue *any* dream if you're tucked away, afraid of exposing yourself? That's not bravery; that's bondage.

Amanda's dilemma is one I have heard confessed more times than I dare admit. When I retrace conversations with the brokenhearted, I find the deepest hurts came from relationships that gradually disintegrated over time. Often, one person would distance himself or herself from the other without explanation or any sign of conflict. This is what happened with Amanda and Reese. And also, just maybe, centuries ago with Peter and Jesus. Small foxes. Epic changes. The line between love and betrayal blurred before anyone could blink.

Coming to grips with the reality that we have not only been victims of betrayal but have also held the knife of injustice in our own hands will help keep us from being accomplices in our own heartache.

But I can't leave you holding the knife without offering grace. Jesus didn't. Peter betrayed Jesus . . . then Jesus restored Peter. That's how grace operates. It substitutes Christ's victory for our failure. In fact, after decades of messy mistakes, I've come to realize that our mess-ups often lead to our greatest breakthroughs. It is usually after our biggest falls that we stop and question whether we have been walking according to our own wills, or according to Christ's. When we realize the truth, it often leads to a repentance that turns our lives around.

This book is all about becoming brave and making others brave. But being brave isn't about being a strong person who never blows it. It's about being a person whom God can pour strength into as it's needed to overcome the messes we make of our lives. *That's* grace. Today, it doesn't matter if you need grace to forgive your betrayer or grace to be forgiven for betrayal. Either way, it is grace that will get you beyond the pain and make you brave, so you can get back on track and pursue your lost dreams.

Betrayal. There probably isn't a more paralyzing word in the English language, so let's talk a little bit more about it before moving on.

Betrayal is the breaking or violation of a contract, a trust, or a confidence that produces moral conflict within a relationship. *Moral conflict.* That's a very nice way of describing our reaction when we discover that the dagger in our back was embedded by someone we once trusted. If you have been betrayed, or worse, you are about to commit an act of betrayal, you may be tempted to shut this book and read one on joy instead. I beg you to reconsider. Confrontation makes us uncomfortable. I get that. But you will never be able to conquer what you are unwilling to address. Running from the truth may give you temporary comfort, but you will gain strength when you face the truth and act on it.

Betrayal is placing bets against your destiny. The stakes are high. Your very dreams are at risk.

Like everyone else, I have watched deception break up a tight-knit circle of friends. Just last month a decade-long friendship ended over an email thread delivered to the wrong in-box.

One click of "Reply to All" divided a group of colleagues. Just for the record, it wasn't just a friendship at stake. These were game changers in a high-profile industry.

If our enemy cannot get us to lay down our swords in frustration, he will get us to turn them on each other. I've had ringside seats to family fallouts. I've watched frivolous arguments turn into free-for-alls that left siblings disconnected for decades.

Even though I'm no longer paranoid about being betrayed, I prefer to keep betrayal at arm's length. Yes, I acknowledge there are benefits to pain. And I've lived long enough to know trouble doesn't last forever. While my mind understands these principles, my heart is prone to tuck tail and run for the cave marked *alienation*.

But I can't hide from life. Neither can you. If the enemy ever isolates us, he has a better chance of destroying us. The adage "There's safety in numbers" isn't just true for wildlife; it's true for us too.

The intertwining of our destinies leaves us powerful and vulnerable all at the same time. I wish that were not the case. I don't mind the "leaves us powerful" part of that clause, but the reference to vulnerability makes me want to tuck into my shell. The longer I live, the stronger I'm convinced that the success of our dreams is more dependent on each other than we have imagined. Our society has done us no greater injustice than creating an independent, go-it-alone, me-first culture. That kind of shallow thinking may make the world proud, but it makes God cringe.

Every time I read these verses, my heart grows soft at the thought of how much we need each other:

If our enemy cannot get us to lay down our swords in frustration, he will get us to turn them on each other.

Two people are better than one,
  because they get more done by working together.
If one falls down,
  the other can help him up.
But it is bad for the person who is alone and falls,
  because no one is there to help.

(Ecclesiastes 4:9–10)

I don't know what dream you're chasing, but it will require assistance from your tribe. But beware: the enemy of your destiny seeks to *infect* those most treasured relationships. To *contaminate* them. He takes pleasure in pulling us away from those who could push us forward toward our dreams. He knows that it is within the safety of our most trusted relationships that our gifts thrive and our potential is maximized. We must not allow him to set us against the very ones who can make us better. We don't have time to waste shooting arrows at each other.

Every fulfilled dream will require the help of someone close to you. Some people will be brought into your life to collaborate with you creatively, some to assist you financially, others to strengthen you emotionally. But when you have a dream, it will attract both helpers and haters. Often the haters will enter your life as helpers, then morph into betrayers. But before we identify the haters, let's catch a glimpse of what a helper looks like.

Vincent Van Gogh is considered one of the most influential figures in Western art history. In just over a decade, the Dutch

Postimpressionist brought to life more than 2,100 works of art, including 860 oil paintings. Most of us would be content creating a handful of creative masterpieces. Not Vincent. But despite his enormous success, his constant struggle to make sense of life left him emotionally and mentally tormented. Haunted by fear that his expressive brushwork was out of sync with the sketches of the day, he despaired of life.

As he considered walking away from the art industry, his brother, Theo, suggested a change of scenery, not for the canvas but for Vincent himself.

Vincent was the paint slinger, but Theo was a well-connected art dealer. He believed in his misfit artist brother enough to move him to Paris and introduce him to a group of free-spirited Impressionists. Theo supported his brother's work when no one understood it. Without Theo's influence on Vincent, the world might have missed looking at *The Starry Night*. Dear friend, please remember you don't have to be the one painting history to change history.

The trickle effect of our influence affects the world in ways we haven't imagined. And as women, our influence on our culture is more impactful today than at any other time in modern history. So when I speak before women, I keep before them this truth: *If we are to live out our destinies, we will have to lean into and look out for each other.* Help each other. And *never* betray each other.

I'm not sure what dream God has placed in your heart, but I offer these words of wisdom: wherever there is a dreamer, there will be dream destroyers. In fact, it is not uncommon for friends to turn into rivals the moment dreams begin to flourish. I wish I could delete that last line. I can't. It's true.

Bundling dreams and relationships together is like building a house out of playing cards. Although it may look secure, one wobbly bump of the table and down it tumbles. I'm sure you've had your cards fall too. How did you react when you were betrayed or rejected? Did you lose faith in people? Did it rattle your trust in God? Was it epic enough to make you retreat into seclusion? Did it leave you believing your dreams were nothing more than delusions? If so, you have played right into the dream thief's hands.

> It is not uncommon for friends to turn into rivals the moment dreams begin to flourish.

Just a few weeks ago, an unexpected fallout with a friend had me restacking my freshly collapsed house of cards. My heart refused to be comforted, and there was no way to convince myself that anything beautiful could come from such betrayal. The truth was, it was time for me to move on. Some relationships are meant to end, but if you're like me, you may tend to hang on to people longer than you should.

If we are not careful, our grief will have us reaching back for the very ones who betrayed us rather than looking ahead for who God may be sending to help us take back our stolen dreams.

Most of us love the thought of miracles. Even the way the word slips off our lips feels good. *M-m-miracles.* But what happens when God uses something unpredictable to set the stage for our miracle? We pray for miracles, but if we knew they would come packaged in unfaithfulness, deception, or double-crossing, would we still unwrap them? I doubt it.

Years ago, a good portion of our daughter's college tuition came wrapped in a package of middle school bullying. After months of backstabbing, betrayal, and threats, our daughter transferred schools during winter break. We had no idea she would transfer just in time to enter a scholarship program awarding her 70 percent of her college tuition. I still smile when I think about the circumstances. Bullying actually positioned her for a blessing. Isn't that like God, to use our enemies to position us for prosperity?

Middle school girls aren't the only people who can carve out chunks of our hearts. Spouses. Best friends. In-laws. Bosses. The nosy neighbor next door. Any or all of these can betray us, and unless we are intentional about guarding our hearts, the enemy will strip away both our dreams and our self-confidence without us ever knowing they're gone. And not just our *self*-confidence, but confidence in our Father. There are few things more binding than a father-daughter relationship. So it should come as no surprise that from the first day in the garden, our enemy has tried to weaken our confidence in Him. *Why didn't God protect me? Why didn't He warn me? Why did He let someone I loved betray me? Why did He shatter my dreams?*

And the enemy knows that if he can sow discontent in our relationship with our heavenly Father, he can wreck every other relationship we have too. I've yet to meet someone who is angry with God and not angry with other people. The opposite is also true: if we lose confidence in others, whom we can see, then how can we ever trust God, whom we cannot see? Trust issues don't just eat away the foundations of our relationships; they deteriorate our faith in God, in ourselves, and in our dreams. Don't let an act of disloyalty demagnetize your faith compass.

The bottom line is, as long as you live in human skin, you are subject to betrayal. The dream thief is ever on the prowl. The question is, will you let betrayal steal your dreams like stealing a bone from a dog, or . . . will you sink your teeth into those dreams and hang on like a pit bull, refusing to let *anyone* take them from you? I know *just* what you'll do. You'll hang on . . .

FOR

Further Reflection

1. Have the wounds of someone you once considered a *safe sister* kept you from trusting someone new? Who can you think of right now who'd like to be a part of your life, but you're shutting that person out for fear of being hurt?

2. Have you ever been betrayed by a friend, family member, or colleague? If so, how did it affect you? Did you get over it quickly, or are you still nursing your grief? Did that act of betrayal make you stronger? If so, in what ways?

3. Most of us are familiar with Ecclesiastes 4:9–10, but not as many know verses 11 and 12. Read Ecclesiastes 4:12, then think of one or two people with whom you could partner in prayer for each other's dreams.

4. In this chapter, we learned that God used bullying and betrayal at one school to open the door to a scholarship at another school. Obviously God did not engineer the hateful and painful bullying of a child. But He was able to use it to create a beautiful outcome. Think of a time when God used something painful—maybe even betrayal—to set the stage for something miraculous in your life. Can you name a situation that, though hurtful at the time, led you into a better season?

chapter
SIX

MORE THAN A
SPARTAN

In an earlier chapter, I quoted from the 2017 motion picture *Wonder Woman*. Please indulge me as I quote from a scene in another great film that showcases the strength of women.

In an opening scene of *300*,[1] a Persian courier arrives in Sparta to deliver a message to King Leonidas. During the messenger's conversation with the king, Queen Gorgo speaks up and reprimands the courier. Outraged by the queen's effrontery, the messenger says to the king, "What makes this woman think she can speak among men?" Rather than waiting for Leonidas to defend her, the queen steps forward and answers, "Because only Spartan women give birth to real men."[2] That one statement leveled the verbal sparring field and made room for women to speak for themselves in a culture that would keep them silent.

Can you imagine what rating some sections of the Bible would receive if they were played out on the big screen? Based on language, violence, and graphic content, many biblical tales would easily fall in the PG-13 category. The tale of Deborah, briefly discussed earlier, might bump the rating even higher for its warfare and bloodshed, but Deborah's story shows that Spartan women weren't the only ones to step forward and shape history. In the twelfth century BC, Judge Deborah proved she was every bit as fierce as the sheroes of Sparta.

Rather than have you read a wordy version of her tale, I have recreated her story in the form of a screenplay. As we read through this script together, use your senses to connect with the scene. Visualize palm branches waving in the distant background. Feel heat rising from the desert floor. Raise your nose and smell the camels walk by. Close your eyes and taste sand mingled with salty sea air. Lean in and hear synchronized footsteps of soldiers marching north. Are you ready to peer through the frame and watch the battle unfold? Let's look at it together.

Fade in: hill country of Ephraim—sunset
Setting: in the heart of the desert, tall palm trees, camels
lying in the sand
Deborah: judge over Israel
Barak: general over Israel's army
Sisera: antagonist, general in opposing army
Jael: unemployed housewife

SCENE 1

DEBORAH (TO BARAK): It has become clear that God commands you: Go to Mount Tabor and prepare for battle. Take ten companies of soldiers. I'll take care of getting Sisera to the Kishon River with all his chariots and troops. And I'll make sure you win the battle.

BARAK: If you go with me, I'll go. But if you don't go with me, I won't go.

DEBORAH: Of course I'll go with you. But understand that with an attitude like that, there'll be no glory in it for you. God will use a woman's hand to take care of Sisera.

SCENE 2

Deborah and Barak gather the tribes of Naphtali and Zebulun along with ten thousand troops. When Sisera gets word Barak has moved his troops to Mount Tabor, he assembles his entire army, including nine hundred chariots of iron.

DEBORAH (TO BARAK): Charge! This very day God has given you victory over Sisera. He is marching before you.

Barak leaves Tabor with ten thousand warriors following. Standing on a jagged cliff, Barak and his forces watch the Eternal One unleash chaos in the enemy's camp. By sunset all of Sisera's army has fallen by the sword. Only Sisera escapes alive. Climbing out of his chariot, he flees on foot.

SCENE 3

Sisera arrives at the tent of Jael, the wife of Heber the Kenite, whom he believes to be an ally.

JAEL: Welcome, my lord. Come in, come in. You're safe now. There is nothing to be afraid of here.

Sisera follows Jael into the tent.

JAEL: Lie down and rest. I'll keep an eye out.

Sisera lies down on the floor. Jael covers him with a rug in case Barak's soldiers come looking for him.

SISERA: Please, a little water. I'm thirsty.

Jael opens a skin filled with milk and gives him a drink, then covers him up again.

SISERA: Stand at the tent flap. If anyone comes by and asks you, "Is there anyone here?" tell him, "No, not a soul."

Battle weary, Sisera falls into a deep sleep. Jael, now assured he sleeps, quietly retrieves a tent peg and a hammer. She creeps softly to his side and poises the tent peg just over his temple. Then, with force, she drives it through his head and into the ground with her hammer. Sisera dies on impact.

SCENE 4

Barak comes looking for Sisera. Hearing him outside her tent, Jael meets Barak at the tent door.

JAEL: Looking for someone? Come. I'll show you the man you're looking for.

Barak enters the tent and discovers the grisly scene.

Fade away.

Dramatic? Yes. I agree. But I share this tale to remind you that God chose two strong women to headline His script for victory. Given the blood and gore of this story, most directors would have chosen men for the leading roles. Maybe the angels even suggested to the Lord that casting men would make more sense. If they did, their opinions didn't carry any weight with the Producer. God had already cast His leading ladies. He needed a judge to roll the opening scene and a housewife to nail shut the final one.

With great intention God selected women from different occupations and contrasting walks of life to win this battle. Our Father thinks that way. He is willing to include anyone who has a heart to be cast in a history-changing story. There is an epic role for each of us to play, even you. The question is, are you willing to show up for the audition?

I'm sure it never occurred to Deborah or Jael that they would one day be called sheroes. The day before the action began, one wore a judge's robe, the other a house robe. But God invites each of us to be a world changer right where we live.

Can I lay aside the soft talk and speak plainly for a moment? What I am about to share is not a rebuke to our gender but a challenge, a provocation to bump the bar of bravery up a notch or two.

Standing before a group of women in a remote wooded village, I opened our retreat with a series of probing questions. Wanting to get a pulse on the group with whom I would share the weekend, I instructed the women to break into small groups and sit comfortably on the floor. With everyone settled in, I gave the assignment: each person in a group would have five minutes to introduce herself to the rest of her group and share on the topic of *life's most disappointing moment.*

God has an epic role for each of us to play, even you. The question is, are you willing to show up for the audition?

Chatting it up like schoolgirls, the roomful of women unloaded private, painful issues. Trust me when I tell you it took more than a quick minute to dial down the volume and reclaim order. I opened the second round of dialogue by inviting them to share about a relationship that ended painfully. Once again the conversation erupted as strangers swapped stories like sisters.

What happened next was entirely disappointing. For the final assignment, I asked the women to tell of a time when they'd acted courageously.

The oversized cabin grew eerily quiet. For the first time, I could hear the crackle of the fireplace and the hum of the outdated appliances. The women stared at me, then at each other. The silence was louder than thunder.

I'm not sure why the invitation to talk about courage often trips women up.

For the life of me, I can't add together all the hours I've spent mulling over why we can't mesh our names together with the word *courage*. Is it that we've failed to *be* courageous, or do we simply feel unqualified to be *labeled* courageous? Perhaps we cannot call to mind moments of courage because we have had too few.

It seems we women feel more comfortable referring to ourselves as wounded than as warriors. But that's not the case with the men in our lives. Put men around a bonfire and the competition for who has more grit gets heated. As the night passes, the tales get taller and the fables become more fictitious. Men talk about themselves as if they are legends.

Men shouldn't be the only ones swapping long-winded stories of heroism. It would be good for us daughters to think of ourselves as daring too. With a culture in need of moral clarity, our hearts should leap at the idea of leading the charge to liberate those who are blinded and bound by sin. Until we are daunting enough to live up to our God-given title of *brave savior* (see chapter 2), we will live powerless lives marked by forgotten dreams.

Maybe it's my age or where I am in life right now; I'm not sure. But I've simply grown weary of a yo-yo type of bravery. It is with all love that I insist we can't be plucky one day and pitiful the next. The unhealthy habit of swaying between faith and fear will only leave us as mental messes.

If we are to become brave, our words must echo our resolve to step out of the shadows and do something meaningful. I can usually judge how serious a woman is about stretching beyond her comfort zone by the verbal choices she makes in describing her future. Anyone can create a vision board, but it takes a determined woman to create a word board. I challenge you to find a tucked-away corner where you can pin your favorite mottos, inspirational catchphrases, or battle cries. Post them. Confess them. Allow these words to breathe life into your weary soul. Most important, get comfortable speaking out what you desire to live out.

What a woman holds hidden in her heart will eventually tumble out of her mouth. Don't believe me? Have you tried to hold an emotion inside and not let it slip from your lips? Almost impossible. That's because our hearts and our mouths are wired to work in unison. What we say, our hearts believe. And what our hearts believe, we will speak. Jesus Himself said, "People speak the things that are in their hearts" (Luke 6:45). But our words are a double-edged blade. Solomon wrote:

> The words of the reckless pierce like swords,
> but the tongue of the wise brings healing.
> (Proverbs 12:18 NIV)

What we confess about our future is far more significant than any obstacle or enemy we will encounter. Our words are confessions of our internal persuasions. What we continue to confess will become the framework of our future.

What we continue to

confess will become

the framework

of our future.

A wise man once said, "Fairy tales do not tell children that dragons exist. Children already know that dragons exist. Fairy tales tell children that dragons can be killed."[3]

Let's dig deeper into that thought. If a child can be convinced that fire-breathing dragons can be defeated, she can also be convinced that anything else that frightens her can also be defeated. That's how courage is born. Somewhere down deep, children must believe they are able to defeat what frightens them most.

What do you do with your grown-up version of dragons? How do you handle the monsters, the ones that don't have scales but leave scars anyway? What about the ones that don't? They may not breathe fire, but somehow you still feel the burn. Whether you are age four or forty-four, those giants are not easy to confront. The courage to go up against what we most fear often begins with our mouths before it ever gives movement to our feet. Authentic bravery is activated by our vocabulary long before it gives way to action.

Our words have influence over our surroundings. Picture Jesus staring into the face of the storm and speaking the words, "Peace, be still." When those three words rippled over the water, the waves quit cascading over the bow of the boat (Mark 4:36–39 KJV).

So how about you? What words tumble off *your* lips during moments of crisis?

My life never moved in the right direction until my words began to lead the way. When I started speaking life into my future, it took on the shape of those words. Remember, that's how God created the very world we live in. He spoke. The Bible tells us that the "whole world was made by God's *command*"

(Hebrews 11:3, emphasis added). And then, when He created man, we are told that God *breathed* into him, and "man became a living soul" (Genesis 2:7 KJV). Sometimes our dreams just need us to breathe life into them, to speak life into them. What words are you using to shape your future? Are they words God would speak over you? Are they positive? Encouraging? Inspiring? Every word you speak in some way shapes your destiny.

As a woman who has witnessed words shape the lives of my sisters, I urge you to resolve to crush the self-criticism and any other words that would get in the way of your future, and replace them with words of faith. As you change your vocabulary, things will begin to shift in a new direction. Be intentional about verbalizing the future you want to experience.

Now I'd like to relate the story of David and Goliath, but with a modern-day twist. For those of you who haven't read the tale in a while, here is my take on how it all started:

1. A giant (Goliath) tweets out threats against God's people.
2. A teenager (David) reads the giant's threats and tweets back his own threats.
3. King Saul sees the online exchange and asks for an exclusive interview with David.

Granted, Twitter wasn't around in the ninth century BC, but if it had been, a full-on Twitter war would have ensued. What we do know is David's threats against Goliath reached the staff of King Saul. Desperate for anyone bravehearted enough to step up and face the giant, Saul invited David for dinner. David's confidence is captured in 1 Samuel 17:

> "Let no man's heart fail because of [Goliath]. Your servant will go and fight with this Philistine. . . . Your servant used to keep sheep for his father. And when there came a lion, or a bear, and took a lamb from the flock, I went after him and struck him and delivered it out of his mouth. And if he arose against me, I caught him by his beard and struck him and killed him. Your servant has struck down both lions and bears, and this uncircumcised Philistine shall be like one of them, for he has defied the armies of the living God." And David said, "The LORD who delivered me from the paw of the lion and from the paw of the bear will deliver me from the hand of this Philistine." (vv. 32, 34–37 ESV)

Bravehearted people have a way of empowering the timid to face giants that look terrifying. David used his words to weaken the fears of men who were acting more like schoolgirls than soldiers. If he doubted his ability to slay a giant double his height and twice his age, no one knew it.

David's meeting with Saul wasn't a push for publicity but an opportunity to infuse strength into weak leadership.

I can usually tell what will become of someone by how that person treats the outgoing leadership team. It's easy to treat well the rising star, but the grace with which you treat the shooting star says a lot about your character.

Whether David's words were an attempt to encourage himself or win over Saul's opinion wasn't the issue. Too often we get caught up in trying to explain how God is going to bring miracles *to* us and we forget to tell about the miracles He brought *through* us. God isn't looking for us to speak loudly; He's listening to see if we speak with authority. Speaking with authority, David rehearsed how God had given him victory before in sticky situations. And then he boldly stated that God would do the same *again*.

The difference between David and every other man on the battlefield was that they looked for excuses and David looked for opportunity. Every soldier in Saul's army likely sought advancement; yet all of them shrank when the opportunity arose. Some of them

Bravehearted people have a way of empowering the timid to face giants that look terrifying.

may have *wanted* to confront the giant; they just didn't know how. The same could be true for us. Maybe we miss our divine moments not because we don't *want* to try but because we don't even know *how* to try.

There have been moments when I simply didn't know how to put feet to my courage. I was in my early thirties when I felt called to step forward and create a television program. I had the faith to follow where I sensed God was leading, but I needed someone to show me how to put my faith into action. At the right moment, God sent the perfect person to show me how to push forward with my dream. From their example, I began to make decisions that would shape my destiny.

Maybe you need someone to show you how to walk out what is hidden in your heart. Jesus did that for His disciples. He placed *opportunity* before *expectation*. He invited them to *participate* in miracles before asking them to *perform* them. As you move into the next season in life, I ask that God will connect you with the person who will awaken your courage.

There is a moment in everyone's journey when deep-rooted conviction requires us to creep beyond the borders of what is comfortable and into the land of uncertainty. Live long enough and faith will demand that passion bypass passivity, if for no other reason than we were created to trust God. Nothing is more pleasing to our Father than ordinary people who are willing to stretch toward extraordinary things.

God is searching for audacious faith.

We've been discussing *bravery* from the very start of this book. But have you considered the meaning of the word? By definition, bravery is "the ability to confront crisis, danger, or pain despite experiencing the emotion of fear."

At the root of a courageous heart is internal confidence. David had this kind of heart. People like him are easy to recognize. They are the ones, whether on the playground or in the boardroom, who ask, "What happens when I win?" Not, "What happens *if* I fail?" but, "What is my reward *when* I win?" David's wording showed no doubt in his mind that the giant would be killed: "What will be done to reward the man who kills this Philistine?" (1 Samuel 17:26).

If we approach giants without asking about rewards, we may decide to run the other way. Every battle should come with an incentive. When you are willing to fight the giants of our culture, expect a giant-size reward. Whatever battle you're warring through, I encourage you to list what you want once you're on the victory side. Documenting our expectations empowers us to stare down our fears and bet against our circumstances.

Once you put your expectations down on paper, start declaring them, every day. The word *declare* means: (1) to announce officially; (2) to proclaim; (3) to make public the status of a situation.

Today, and every day hereafter, let your declaration of faith overtake any negative emotions and fears. Join me in speaking words of change over your situation. Here are a few to get you started.

Daily Declarations

- I declare that I walk in favor with God and man. *To the measure that I bless and care for others, may God release favor over my life, my family, and my career.*
- I declare that I am wired for success. *I take charge of my mind, thoughts, actions, and reactions. By purposefully engaging my mind with good things, I create a successful future.*
- I declare I am full of wisdom and strength. *I will fuel my mind and body with good things. I walk away from things that would pollute my body or soul. Daily I detoxify my environment, fleeing destructive environments or relationships.*
- I declare healing is mine to receive. *I stand ready to receive physical, emotional, spiritual, mental, and relational healing. Daily I review God's promises to renew any broken area of my life. And I will do my part by thinking stable thoughts and meditating on positive things.*

- I declare that my relationships are stable. *I am mindful of the power of association. I am careful in my selection of those I will confide in and bring into my inner circle.*
- I declare that my business and dreams will thrive. *I expect God to lead me into areas of uncommon increase and prosperity. Daily I prepare to accomplish the dreams hidden in my heart.*
- I declare an overabundance of resources and assets. *Based on my generosity and stewardship of the things I have, I position myself to receive a good return on my finances and wealth.*

By speaking these confessions out loud, we position ourselves to receive the blessings of our Father. He has placed within us creative minds so we can envision our future and brave hearts so we can live out our dreams.

Now I have an assignment for you. I want you to gather your favorite pen and your well-worn journal and settle into the private place where you meet with God. There, alone with Him, I want you to search out whether or not you have a courageous heart. I'm not referring to a casual examination, where you ask yourself easy questions. I want you to splay open your heart and let God show you the real condition of your faith.

It would be fitting while in this intimate atmosphere to make a list of times you have acted like an *ezer* (see chapter 2). Archive those moments when you cast off shame, picked up grace, and moved forward with a brave heart. List the courageous choices you have made. Did you choose to forgive and heal rather than settle for a broken marriage? To carry a child rather than seek abortion? To rise up from the ashes of depression rather than wallow in despair? Or to successfully launch a business when others said it was impossible? Revisit these moments and record them.

Write as much as you can in whatever way reflects your journey. Color in the margins. Write in loopy longhand. Scribble. Scrawl. Just be honest about the demonstrations of your courage and the current condition of your heart. If, when you place your pen down, there is more blank space than filled-in space, I want you to find where your courage has been hiding—and why. If you will take the time, I am confident you will not only rediscover your courage, you will reclaim it . . .

Because you were created brave.

Further Reflection

1. No matter our status or occupation, God invites each of us to be a world changer right where we live. How is your influence affecting those you connect with on a daily basis? More specifically, has someone in your circle made a bold, courageous move because of your encouragement? If so, who was it, and in what way did that individual demonstrate his or her courage? What words did you speak that summoned up that person's courage to take that step?

2. Read Proverbs 12:18 from the NIV. Then think a moment about your self-talk. Are the words you use about yourself "reckless"? Do they "pierce like swords"? Or do they "bring healing"? Now read James 3:10, preferably out of the King James Version or the NASB (you can find all these versions on BibleGateway.com). Would you consider your self-talk to be more blessing or cursing? What words of *faith* do you use to describe your future?

3. Revisit the story of David in this chapter, or read his story in the Bible (1 Samuel 17). Now think about a challenge you are facing. How different might the outcome be if you go into the challenge assuming victory and expecting rewards? What rewards are you seeking for overcoming this challenge?

4. Earlier I said that maybe you need someone to show you *how* to walk out what is hidden in your heart. Is there a dream

tucked away that you're courageous enough to pursue, but you don't even know where to start? Who could you turn to for direction? Is there someone you know who has already succeeded at or has inside knowledge of what you would like to achieve? If so, are you willing to be mentored by that individual? Are you brave enough to ask?

chapter SEVEN

THE QUEST

Quietly, quickly, Jehosheba crept down the marble steps and made her way to the stables. There wasn't time for weepy-eyed embraces or drawn out goodbyes. She would miss the rhythm of the castle, the lighthearted laughter, the amenities that opulent living provided. But right now those thoughts were pushed far into the background. She was on a holy mission, and that mission was to ensure that her infant son, Joash,[1] survived the beheadings.

The days leading up to the coup could only be described as gruesome. After King Ahaziah's assassination, Queen Athaliah began to massacre the entire royal family. Jehosheba had witnessed the wrath of this wicked woman for generations; she knew how this would play out. So, clutching Joash tightly to her chest, Jehosheba mounted her horse, and they fled into the forest.

Soaked from the morning dew, the weary two arrived at the temple at dawn. It was there, within the temple walls with the high priest, that the infant prince would be safe.

---

1 Some Bible versions translate this *Jehoash*.

For six years Prince Joash remained hidden in the temple. Then, as if scripted for a feature film, the plot took an erratic turn. Tucked away in the ancient manuscript of 2 Kings are these words: *In the seventh year, following the death of Athaliah, Prince Joash ascended to the throne of Judea* (11:4, 20–21, paraphrased).

Note that while Joash became the hero of the story (2 Kings 12), it was his aunt who made the story possible by saving the future king's life. Every great story of heroism begins with risk long before it ends in reward. That is true whether in a novel, a screenplay, or the script of your life.

To *love* is to risk. And Jehosheba was willing to risk her life out of love for another.

The whole world is on a quest for love. We all desire it. Men fight for it. Women crave it. Children die without it. In light of that universal need, the most beautiful act any woman can perform is to immerse those around her in love.

But love comes with a risk. My prayer is for every daughter of the King to rise up and risk loving, and not just loving those who make it easy. Love those who are difficult and near-impossible to love, those who have hurt you, and even those who have betrayed you. It takes a great deal of nerve to love someone who betrays our trust. We have to almost wear blinders to overlook some of the ridiculous actions of those who break faith with us. And we'd rather not. We all want to be loved, but we don't want love to hurt, so we withhold love. We're a complex crowd. Frightened of being unloved, yet afraid to love. Down deep we find it difficult to give away what we crave most. And yet, it has been wisely observed that loving someone deeply and unconditionally gives you courage.

I understand that not every loving and courageous act has a castle for a backdrop. Sometimes it's a plane. And not every courageous act involves saving someone's life; it could just mean helping her find healing and strength. And daring to show her love.

> It takes a great deal of nerve to love someone who betrays our trust.

Not long ago, I threw my carry-on in the overhead bin and slid into seat 15B. My first flight had been canceled and my second flight was hours behind schedule. I needed rest and wanted space. As cold as this may seem, I prayed that whoever had reserved 15A would be a no-show.

As the cabin lights dimmed and the door was about to shut, in walked a young woman wearing ripped jeans and a charcoal-gray hoodie.

Down the aisle she came before stopping at my row. "Excuse me. I'm 15A."

My heart sank. The sigh that escaped my lips must have escaped more loudly than I thought, as the man across the aisle smirked and said, "Thought ya had it made, didn't ya?"

Passenger 15A was tall and thin. She looked like a model. Although she tried to get comfortable, her long legs didn't quite fit into the tiny space between the seats. In fact, nothing about her seemed comfortable. I don't just mean the lanky giraffe legs. But the way she stared wistfully out the window, her fingers fidgeting. There was something somber, almost dark about her countenance.

Halfway into the flight, I noticed tears slide down her cheeks. I could tell by the way she flung them away that they weren't just sad tears but bitter ones. As hard as I had prayed for her to be a no-show on the flight, I now prayed even harder for God to give me an opportunity to reach her wounded soul.

Her name was Amber, I learned. Before long I knew her story too. Amber was traveling back from visiting her father at NJSP. I asked what the acronym stood for and she spelled it out: New Jersey State Prison. He was an LWOP, she said. That was another acronym I would need help with. It means life without possibility of parole. Thankfully, I didn't have to ask his crime; she volunteered it: murder. In fact, at age eight, Amber had watched him murder her mother.

Family had tried to convince Amber it was an accident, a drunken fight that had escalated out of control. She's still not sure how it all unraveled. What she does know is that after her mother's brutal death and her father's incarceration, life didn't get any better. She was sexually abused by her uncles for years. As a preteen, she was taken to hotels and sold for sexual favors. I will spare you the graphic details; they are far too disturbing to repeat.

Two hours into her story, Amber gently leaned in and asked, "Why do I feel these horrible things are my fault? I try to push back the memories, but they keep replaying in my mind."

As our flight descended, I took the moments we had left to share how God longed to knit her heart back together. I took a running leap of faith and lovingly shared about a heavenly Father who would never leave or abandon or abuse His daughter. She seemed to relax a bit. I could tell the Holy Spirit was gently setting her free, like a cork being released from a bottle.

I pushed forward and shared how God didn't breathe life into us to let us be swallowed up by its tragedies. No, He gave us life because He loves us and has never stopped thinking about us. As I continued sharing, her tears kept flowing. But now the bitter tears were turning into being-made-better tears. The Father was embracing His daughter, and she was responding to His love.

Funny, but though she may not have known it, Amber had been on a quest for love—real love, a Father's love. We are all searching for our Father's love. For those of us who have found it, let's have the courage to help our sisters find it too.

I just want to pause here for a moment and talk with you about cutting loose people who systematically strip away your courage. Letting go of people who continue to let you down or bring you down is not only necessary; it is liberating.

Let me tell you about my friend Sydney. A few months back, she sent me this email. (The unnecessary details have been removed):

> For about ten years I've remained trapped in a broken friendship. At least it's been fractured on my end of things. Cheri and I became friends through work. We were hired about the same time, and Cheri quickly set her eyes on a managerial position. Over time she worked her way to the corporate office. She climbed. I was her cheerleader. It's not that I didn't have aspirations of my own. They just ended up in the wake of what

was important to Cheri. I can't explain how our relationship found its way to such an unhealthy place. Perhaps I
was so content going with the flow that I failed to notice
how far off script my life had drifted.

I wish Sydney's email were one of a kind. It's not. Just yesterday at the gym, my phone pinged as a series of texts came
tumbling through. A friend I've worked with for years sent me
cut-and-paste texts from her fiancé. Engaged a week and he
was already asking her to check her dreams at the door and
dive headlong into his. She asked what I thought she should
do. Sigh. I wanted to slide right off the treadmill and scream.
My frustration was not with her but with him, and with self-
entitled people in general. It is wearisome to watch sisters of
our tribe abandon dreams God has locked away in their hearts
because they get swept away feeling they should always play second chair. If we don't pay close attention, our dreams can get
tossed into the back seat and driven down the road of someone
else's journey.

The actions and reactions of those we commit to *doing life* with
play a large role in whether we experience the rush of running
headlong into life or feel paralyzed by the daily grind. The
other day I arrived late to spin class and found someone had
taken my spot. Forced to find a bike at the back of the room,
I landed next to a woman who looked close to my age. By the
time I'd settled into the saddle, the music was pulsing and the
class had fallen into a rhythmic stride.

I knew what was coming: warm-up, followed by a steady mix of up-tempo cadences, sprints, climbs, and then a moderate cooldown. Yep. Bouncing to the beat of the music, I zipped right through the first half hour. But somewhere during the sprint section, I felt sharp pains pass through the center of my knee. Cringing a little, I kept pushing the pedals. I didn't want the woman next to me to think I couldn't keep up. Especially when she was crushing it on BPMs (beats per minute). Don't get me wrong; I wasn't trying to outdo her, but neither did I want her to outdistance me.

I wouldn't describe myself as slightly competitive; that wouldn't be true. I am extremely competitive. Not in a way that is unhealthy or interferes in my relationships. But the kind of competitiveness that makes me almost come unglued when I feel as if I am losing ground or coming up short. And falling behind was exactly what I was doing. In an effort to regain lost ground, I made a slight adjustment. The only problem was, the way I adjusted worsened my already weakened knee.

By this point in life I've officially lost count of how many times the fear of falling behind has caused me to lose sight of my dreams. It's not always the unambitious that end up underachieving; sometimes the person who fights hardest loses ground because her eyes drift out of her lane.

Anyone who has ever tried to tiptoe over a balance beam knows the secret to not falling is to become good at spotting. Spotting involves nothing more than focusing on an eye-level object across the room. By keeping your eyes fixed on what is in front of you, your feet instinctively follow the direction you are looking. A quick sideways glance at the girl beside you is the quickest way to lose your balance and footing.

Before we push on to something new, let's bring the topics of hurts and dreams to the same table. I honestly don't think we can move ahead until we connect the two. If their roots weren't so deeply intertwined, I wouldn't take up a second of our time. But we need to dig up a few issues to clear the path for our future.

While scanning the internet the other day, I read an interesting blog post. The lead-in line read, "A creeping menace is taking over the planet's tropical forests."

Interested enough to keep reading, I found out that *lianas*, a type of climbing vine, wrap themselves around the trunks of trees and slither their way up to the top branches. Once on top, they create an intertwining canopy pulling water and sunlight away from the trees. They not only suck up the resources of the forest, but they are also non-contributors. Unlike trees, which take in volumes of carbon dioxide and then release volumes of oxygen, these thin vines do little to give back to the environment.[1]

Life is filled with *liana* kinds of people. Climbers. Oxygen-suckers. Non-contributors. If we are going to see our dreams flourish, we must disentangle ourselves from people who will climb right over us to soak up resources. I'm not saying we shouldn't help each other out on the way up. What I am doing is cautioning you to watch out for climbers capable of sucking the life out of your dreams.

As you know, though, smart, gifted people are not exempt from relationships that go wrong. Speaking at a conference in Washington this summer, I met Tyra, CEO of a major branding company in Colorado. Over a cup of coffee, she shared the drama she went through when a colleague forged her name on illegal documents, stealing more than $200,000 in assets. It took three years and $40,000 in legal fees to clean up the mess.

After hearing the whole story, I asked Tyra, "How was she able to move around that much money without anyone noticing?" Her response continues to linger in my heart: "It wasn't that she hid away the assets; she simply rearranged them right in front of our eyes. We were blind to the obvious."

When it comes to protecting our dreams, we can fall into the same trap as Tyra. Blinded by what we don't want to see.

Looking back over this chapter and our discussion of the quest for love versus the quest for dominance and glory brings back a childhood memory that, in its own way, makes a great point that we'd do well to remember.

When I was seven, I remember going to the beach with my friend Val, who lived down the street. The first part of the day was perfect. We splashed in the water until our cheeks were burned from the summer sun. At lunch we ate sandwiches and soft-serve ice cream. When the picnic was packed away, we grabbed our plastic shovels and began scooping out sand that would shape our castles. Moats were dug. Drawbridges designed. Towers made tall—or as tall as any seven-year-old could make them.

Everyone was happy. It was the perfect playdate—until Val asked her dad which castle looked the best. Her dad, like any good dad, found something positive to say about each of our castles. He complimented Val's drawbridge design, and he praised the moat around my tower. "You girls both did a great job," he said. "I like them both. They are different, but *equally good*."

With those words I watched Val's expression change, and not for the better. Clearly, those weren't the words she wanted to hear. Dropping her head, she muttered, "Who cares about sandcastles anyway?" And with a broad swipe of her hand, she leveled our castles to the ground. Val had wanted singular approval—and singular glory. *Exclusive* glory.

Seven-year-olds aren't the only ones addicted to approval and scrabbling for glory. We saw the same thing in Sydney and Cheri's story. And I can't tell you how many times I've watched thirty-year-olds tear down each other's dream because each wanted *exclusive* glory, not *shared* glory.

Let me remind you that we are here on this earth for a purpose. And that purpose is to build God's kingdom. We do that by sowing love, not hate. Compassion, not competition. And we do it for *God's* glory, not our own: "If you do anything," advised the apostle Paul, "do it all for the glory of God" (1 Corinthians 10:31).

But back to the sandcastle, allow me to let my imagination run free for a moment. What if Val had said the unthinkable: "Hey, let's put our castles *together*." What if she'd opened up that moat and added some sand and stretched that castle toward mine? And what if, a half hour later, we didn't have two castles, but one great *big*, imposing one? How much more formidable would *that* have been?

It's time we get over our need to be the only one snatching up success. If we are serious about reaching our dreams, we must work together, helping one another. And if we are serious about building God's kingdom, for His glory, it will require us to link our castles together, or more plainly, to join hands and join forces, seek out the broken, pour out our love to them, and make a difference in a lost and hurting world.

Now, *that's* a quest.

Speaking of connecting our "castles," let's talk a little bit more about the power of connection.

A few decades ago, our gender fought with men for the handful of jobs made available to women. Now women have gone from fighting men for a piece of the pie to fighting *each other* over who will own the bakery. But the great leaps we women have made from employees to CEOs will have little impact in a broken world if we don't learn to work better together. Why is that so important? Let me give you an example from nature.

If you were to visit the African Serengeti, you might be surprised to occasionally notice an ostrich walking alongside a zebra. That's right. In the wide-open range, the odd-looking pair stick together like glue. Opposite in nature, their only commonality is that they share the same predators. Stay with me on this thought.

Zebras have a great sense of smell and hearing, but they have poor eyesight. Conversely, while the ostrich has great vision, it cannot hear well. So, rather than each fighting for survival on its own, together they form a symbiotic relationship that keeps them safe from lions on the hunt. In traveling together and warning each other when danger is near, each benefits from the other's strength, and both survive.[2] Taking that one step further, not only do they survive, but each one flourishes in its own way. The zebra will get what it needs; the ostrich will do the same. Neither has to sacrifice its desires or future.

What if, as women, we decided to journey together? How different would the journey be if we chose to defend and protect one another rather than expose one another's vulnerabilities and fight for position? What if we allowed our sisters to flourish and achieve their dreams, instead of undermining one another in our struggle for supremacy? *Nothing* pushes me away from a relationship faster than hearing a woman undermine another sister.

A couple of weeks ago, a lady stopped by the office to talk to me about an idea she had for a project. Fewer than ten minutes into her pitch, she made the fatal mistake of spinning the conversation in a way that made a mutual friend look bad. The younger me would have let her keep rambling. I didn't. I've evolved. I stopped the presentation and explained that though I liked the idea, I didn't like her approach. The project itself would have been perfect for our nonprofit; I just wasn't interested in bringing along a sister who could turn into a predator. I already have a predator. So do you, and he's out to get us. To steal our dreams. To hijack our courage. And shut us down. How much easier are we making the enemy's job when we, as the apostle Paul put it, "bite and devour each other" (Galatians 5:15 NIV)?

We were made to work *together*, in symbiosis. And that, believe it or not, takes courage. It is the brave woman who can work alongside another woman without worrying that her "competitor" will get the credit or the glory. And it is the courageous woman who can applaud her sister's achievements rather than envy them, fear them, or try to outshine them.

So, let's work together. There are hurting hearts out there. Like Sydney's and Amber's. Like your friends' and mine. Let's be the agents who heal those broken hearts.

How different would the journey be if we chose to defend and protect one another rather than expose one another's vulnerabilities?

One final thought as we close out this chapter: it concerns sharing.

When I read the stories of successful women, they all trace back to women helping other women. And we women do that best by sharing what we've learned with one another.

An interesting group study revealed that we are better at taking in new information if we are expected to teach what we have learned to someone else. We organize it better in our minds, remember it more accurately, and retain more selectively the most important parts of what we've learned.

One study divided its participants into two groups. Both groups were given the same information, but facilitators told one group they would simply be tested on the information they were learning. They told the other group that they would have to teach what they'd learned.

In the end, neither group was really required to teach what they'd learned to anyone else, but both groups were tested. Tellingly, the subjects who *thought* they would be required to teach others performed better on the test. The study found that "learning with the idea that we will have to teach the information later tends to invoke better methods of learning subconsciously."[3]

Life is not a test. It's a shared learning experience.

When I think back over the most difficult seasons in my life, I understand those experiences weren't just for my own spiritual growth. The stories that came from hard-pressed places would become life and breath to sisters who would walk the same road.

Over dinner one night, a friend I had known for more than a decade shared a private story that shook me to the core. I couldn't believe there was such a painful chunk of her life that no one knew about. As she related the stickier parts of her story, I tried not to react. I knew it wasn't easy for her to let loose of something that had been held private for so long.

By the time she'd finished telling me the tale, I could see how God's grace and redemption were woven through what would have otherwise been an impossible situation. As tears of release splattered onto my friend's plate, my thoughts drifted to another sister who was going through a similar situation. Unlike my friend who had reached the victory part of her story, this sister was still entangled in the shell-shocked part of her saga.

Before we cleared the dinner plates, I told my friend about the sister who was currently facing the crisis that she had already overcome. Without waiting for me to make the suggestion, my friend gently asked, "Would you mind if I reached out to her?"

Tears of joy formed at the corners of my eyes. And that night I connected two new friends. I hope the healing that one sister experienced and shared has pulled the other sister away from the ledge.

If we are not sharing the secrets we have learned along the journey, then our miracles begin and end with us. But our Father created us to be more than just consumers. We were meant to be *saviors*. Take a moment to think back to what it means to be an *ezer*. An *ezer* is a *helper*, a woman created to *rescue*, to *save*. Whom could you *help* by relating your experiences? Whom could you *rescue* by sharing your stories of God's grace and restoration when all hope seemed lost? Whom could you *save* by instilling hope and courage in her heart and warning her of disastrous outcomes if she stays on her current path? That's what being an *ezer* is all about, and it requires bravery and vulnerability. And love.

In the book of Titus, we are reminded that God has appointed us to pour wisdom into one another. We are to *teach* one another:

> *Teach older women* to be holy in their behavior, not speaking against others or enslaved to too much wine, but teaching what is good. Then *they can teach* the young women to love their husbands, to love their children, to be wise and pure, to be good workers at home, to be kind, and to yield to their husbands. Then no one will be able to criticize the teaching God gave us. (2:3–5, emphasis added)

Did you read that last line carefully? The reason we are to teach and develop one another is so that we *all*, no matter our ages, will exhibit such a sweetness of character that it will allow no room for anyone—especially our enemy—to criticize the teaching God has entrusted to us. Jesus commanded, "Love each other in the same way I have loved you" (John 15:12 NLT). And indeed, the world is on a *quest* for love. They will find no greater love than in the gospel. But nothing will turn them away from the gospel message as quickly as a messenger who doesn't walk the walk. As in every generation past, our faith remains under the microscope of culture. The world is watching how we treat one another. Let's not give them any reason to criticize the good news. Live a life of love—and teach your sisters to do the same.

There *is* an answer to the world's quest for love: it's Jesus. But the world can't see Him, so let them see Him in you. There is no greater act of bravery than that.

FOR

Further Reflection

1. Thinking back to Amber's story, reflect on your own past experiences. Have you ever encountered someone who was clearly upset or broken and who needed a listening ear? How did you respond—or did you? When you see such hurting people, do you tend to engage them and help them or turn the other way, pretending you don't notice?

2. Now think about Sydney and Cheri's story. Are you friends with someone who takes, takes, takes but contributes nothing to the relationship? (Hopefully it's not you!) How can you, in love, confront that friend? If you already have, and it had no effect, might it be time to cut that person loose? How do you go about that?

3. When has a desire for exclusive glory led you to act in a way you regret? Did it result in the loss of a friend, a job, or maybe even a marriage? Are you brave enough to share your story with someone you see walking that same path? What advice can you give her to avoid the same regrets?

4. When I shared with a friend that another sister was experiencing a crisis similar to one she had already overcome, my friend didn't hesitate to get in touch with that hurting sister and share her story of trauma and triumph. Like exposing our weaknesses and our mistakes, sharing our messy or tragic

tales can be painful and leave us feeling vulnerable. But are you willing to share your story anyway, if it means bringing healing to someone who is suffering as you did but can't yet see the light at the end of the tunnel?

chapter
EIGHT

IT'S ALL ABOUT TIMING

I ran my fingers around the edge of my watch and thumped the crystal lens. No response. I unclasped it from my wrist and shook it. Still nothing. Ugh. Somewhere between Times Square and a diner on Canal Street, the quartz movement had suddenly stopped. Frustrated, I began to second-guess my purchase. Beneath the nice crystal face was the word *Rolex*, but as I retraced the conversation I'd had with the street vendor in China Town, I began to doubt its authenticity. Worse, I had no way of knowing what time it was. So how could I possibly get where I was going on time? How frustrating!

Frustration is not an easy word to say. Even the way the syllables roll off our tongues makes it seem uninviting. After watching things we've had high expectations for suddenly fall apart, we feel frustrated. And the emotional toll of not getting what we want can make us downright weary.

Every dream will be threatened by a season of frustration.

Where we allow that frustration to take us will determine what becomes of our dreams. If we stay stuck in the mire of disappointment, we will lose our enthusiasm to live out our passion. We may even lose our way in this maze called life and start living out someone else's passion. It's all too easy to end up somewhere we never intended to go.

Courtney, a thirty-year-old mom of three, knows exactly what that's like. She's living someone else's dream.

It's not that Courtney doesn't appreciate the life she has now; she does. Her husband, Drew, is a corporate attorney, and they live on a beautiful ranch outside of Cherry Creek, Colorado. Most people would be envious of their lifestyle. Their family estate is quite comfortable, but not in a pretentious kind of way. Most of the time, Courtney is genuinely happy, but there are times she feels empty on the inside. She often lies awake at night, imagining what her life would look like if she had pursued her passion, which was fashion design.

Her parents had been opposed to her dreams from the start. They wanted her to *live* fashionably but didn't want her to be the fashion designer. Courtney, frustrated with their lack of support and never good at conflict anyway, did what most young women are taught to do: she settled. She settled into marriage. She settled into a community. She settled for her mother's dreams. She settled into a life that is secure and comfortable—and that is exactly why she is so uncomfortable. She lacks a challenge. She has lost her vision. And she's all but given up on her dream.

If we are not intentional about mapping out our dreams, someone will map them out for us. And most of the time, when others do the planning, we end up failing. Early in life, when

I first started pursuing my dreams, I experienced opposition. *How frustrating!* So, naturally, I tried to become the person others expected me to be. In an effort to please people, I endeavored to accomplish things for which I wasn't wired for success, instead of waiting for the proper time to accomplish what I was gifted to do. For a season, I neglected what I was good at just to appease others. Not only did I end up wasting my time on pursuits for which I was destined to fail, but I stood in the way of someone who was called to succeed.

If we are not intentional about mapping out our dreams, someone will map them out for us.

Over tea and a muffin, my young friend Heather confided how much she disliked her job. A natural creative, she resented the entrapment of her five-by-ten cubicle. Not a day slipped by when she didn't imagine herself perched in front of an art easel, smock smothered in splattered paint.

As our conversation rambled, it was clear she envied her friends who had taken the less-secure route, diving into their passion. There was Sammy, who had a thriving boutique; Jasmine, who skipped across the globe as a travel blogger; and Kallie, who owned a dive shop at the local marina. Sure, each of them had encountered growing pains while expanding the borders of their dreams. They'd experienced their share of bruises, but they never let go of their dreams. They earned the freedom to explore their ambitions.

Heather longed to do the same. For months she had eyed a tucked-away attic space in the arts district. It was a dream spot for opening an art academy and gallery. The arts district had never been more popular, so the timing to launch her dream couldn't have been more perfect. But the nagging what-ifs were keeping her chained to a more conventional way of life. The dreams that longed to fly remained grounded by skepticism, excuses, and indecision.

Here's the problem: the longer we come up with excuses for not stepping out in faith, the more negative outcomes we will imagine. Then we'll *never* step out in faith.

But step out we must, for if we don't, we will be consigned to a life without passion and purpose. To be quite honest, I am frustrated by how quickly we cave in to our fears. When I wrote the book *Downside Up*, I shared in-depth truths on how to release failure and embrace the future. As important as those principles are, I want to dig down a few layers and unearth a deeper thought: *Most women aren't afraid of living. They are terrified of not living out their potential.*

We must fight hard for our futures. Most of us are old enough to know what we want from life. More important, we know what God wants from us. It's time we go from the playground to the battleground.

Let's take a little detour here to discuss a couple of other important topics. On a game show the other night, men were asked to complete the following sentence:

Women have a reputation for _____.

When left to fill in the phrase, guess what the men's top two answers were? They said:

- Women have a reputation for *being unable to make up their minds.*
- Women have a reputation for *being stubborn.*

It's always interesting to see how men view our gender. I'm not saying their assessment was wrong. If anything, they hit the bull's-eye. For thousands of years, we women have held tight to our reputations of being both indecisive and strong willed. I'm not pointing out these traits because they need to be fixed, but so we can better understand ourselves.

Takeko Nakano's story is one to consider.

In ancient Japan, honor and glory were reserved for male soldiers only, making the story of Takeko Nakano remarkable. Not only was she a female Japanese warrior; she was joined by several hundred other samurai warrior women whose complete dedication and extensive suffering remain one of the world's greatest untold stories.[1]

Nakano's determination to become a martial arts master liberated all women of her time to protect and defend their culture.

Let me give you one more example of strong-willed women who took their commitments to a history-making extreme.

After two centuries of Chinese rule, the Vietnamese rose up against them under the leadership of two sisters, Trung Trac and Trung Nhi. Together, they trained thirty-six women to be generals, gathered an army of eighty thousand, and drove the Chinese out of Vietnam in AD 40. Trung Trac would go on to be named ruler, or "She-king Trung."[2]

I am sure very few, if any of us, will become samurai warriors. But that shouldn't keep us from learning a few of their secrets that will serve us in our own pursuits.

Here's what I discovered about the samurai that made them so ferocious on the battlefield. Samurai armor, unlike European armor, was designed for mobility rather than aesthetics. A good suit of armor had to be sturdy yet flexible enough to allow the warrior to maneuver around the battlefield. Made of lacquered plates, the armor was bound together by leather laces, the warrior's arms protected by large, rectangular shoulder shields with light, armored sleeves.

Ornate and decorative, the most interesting part of the samurai armor was the kabuto helmet. Made of riveted metal plates, it looped behind the head, protecting the face and brow. Many helmets also featured ornaments and attachable accessories, including a mustachioed mask that both protected the face and frightened the enemy.[3]

Let's be honest: *When was the last time we frightened our enemy?* If we are to win the battles we all face, we must put on our armor. Not glamorous armor, the kind that makes a fashion statement, but intimidating, battle-worthy armor. (To learn more about the armor of God, read Ephesians 6:10–17.)

Let's take our discussion of armor a step further. Walking through the mall one day, I noticed two athletic stores located side by side. Without calling out the brands, I assure you, one label was made for women who wanted to *work out* in the gym. The other was for women who wanted to *walk around in* the gym. Looking at these different clothing styles in the gym, it's not hard to tell which women will pursue improved fitness and which women just want to look good pretending.

Similarly, it doesn't take much effort for the enemy to identify which women are spiritually ready for war and which women will fall after the first round of fire. Although the enemy cannot read your mind, he can read your reactions. How we react to situations is often a dead giveaway to our lack of confidence. Maybe that is why the samurai refused to go into battle without their masks firmly in place. If they were frightened, no one else would know it.

I'm not suggesting we wear "masks" to try to hide our issues from each other. That's not what we're discussing here. If anything, we need to be more up front and authentic about problems we've held private. I am cautioning you to not react to situations in such a way as to give the enemy any ammunition to use against you. To avoid that mistake, you must put on a brave face and grab your armor. Your sword. Your shield. Your helmet. Protect your head (your mind). Guard your heart—and especially, guard your tongue. And that brings us to another critical topic for discussion here. The tongue.

We talked before about the power of our words, but I can't stress enough how important it is to carefully *weigh out* our words. Let me give you an example of how *not* to use your words:

A friend and I were enjoying a nice, long lunch at the beach. Seated on the patio, we were munching on an assortment of appetizers and poking at salads in cheap wire baskets.

But throughout the meal, my friend kept nervously checking her phone. Concerned, I asked, "Is everything all right?" She replied, "Ugh. I'm frustrated. I put a bid in for a building downtown on Tuesday and haven't heard back from them yet. The space is the exact size I've been praying would come available . . . but I know I probably won't get it. It doesn't matter how hard I try; nothing seems to fall in place for me."

Although the enemy cannot read your mind, he can read your reactions.

Her words struck a nerve. I began to think about my own life and how many times I have spoken faith in the first part of a sentence, only to communicate doubt in the last half of the sentence. We are a sad lot if we cannot hold on to our faith for a sentence or two. It's time we get serious about what we are saying. If our faith is bold enough to believe for something, our mouths should be consistent enough to carry that faith forward. That or we should say nothing at all.

We may not see any possible way that what we hope for could ever come to pass. But we dare not speak it. The Bible tells us that when we ask Him for something, we must believe and not doubt, "because the one who doubts is like a wave of the sea, blown and tossed by the wind. That person should not expect to receive anything from the Lord" (James 1:6–7 NIV). We need to latch on to hope as a samurai latches on to her sword, and fight for what we're believing for. And even if the odds seem stacked against us, we mustn't utter *one word* to suggest that we expect anything less than victory. That's what faith is all about:

Now faith is the assurance that what we hope for will come about and the certainty that what we cannot see exists. (Hebrews 11:1 ISV)

We have a promise straight from God's Word that if we believe that we have *already* received the things we ask for in prayer (even though we haven't yet seen them), God *will* give them to us (Mark 11:24). That's a promise.

But remember: promises aren't always fulfilled right when we want them to be . . .

At a women's conference in North Carolina, I shared a message on prophetic promises. I realize most of us are mature enough to understand God's plans don't always fit into our time frames. It's not that we have trouble waiting; it's *how* we wait that highlights our insecurities.

The other day I did a background study of women who raised prophetic children. On one side of the paper, I listed the social history of the mother; on the other side, the accomplishments of her children. Topping the list were the following women:

SARAH: Mother of Isaac
ELIZABETH: Mother of John the Baptist
HANNAH: Mother of Samuel
WIFE OF MANOAH: Mother of Samson
RACHEL: Mother of Joseph

As I studied the backstories of these women, I was shocked to see a familiar thread woven throughout each of their stories: the prophetic sons listed above all came from mothers who had barren wombs. Yes, that thought makes me pull in my breath as well.

As I took a few days and thought deeper on the discovery, I became aware that God reserves some wombs for special assignments. What others write off as *barren*, God labels *special reserve*.

What does barrenness have to do with prophecy? More than we might imagine. In biblical days barrenness was viewed as a curse. A woman who couldn't have children was viewed as being out of favor with God. It's the same today, only not necessarily with regard to children. People put pressure on us to "birth" certain things at the same rate they are delivering them. When we can't, they judge us as faithless, unfruitful, or apathetic. There is this unspoken tension between women that whispers, *If we can't keep up, are we at risk of losing our value?*

I remember a season in my early thirties when everyone in my inner circle was giving birth to their dreams. One friend opened a business, another finished a novel, and a third went on tour with her band. It's never easy to be the only one not wearing spiritual maternity clothes. I didn't understand at the time that anything of a prophetic nature is set apart for a specific season. The word *prophetic* simply means something declared by a prophet, especially a divinely inspired prediction, instruction, or exhortation. The book of Ecclesiastes supports that: "There is an appointed time for everything. And there is a time for every event under heaven" (3:1 NASB).

If we are not careful, our drive to see our dreams come to

pass before their time can turn our daydreams into nightmares. Let me walk you through an example.

During the Christmas break I met with Madison, a young friend of mine. As I rounded the corner, I could tell something wasn't quite right. The last time we were together, we had enjoyed flipping through her phone, picking out bridesmaid dresses. I hoped this meeting wasn't going to bring bad news with it. But I wasn't completely caught off guard when it did.

For weeks Madison had been into it with her fiancé, Austin. They argued all the time over whether to move the wedding date closer to spring or leave it as planned for late fall. Madison wanted to speed things up and get married right after college graduation. For financial reasons Austin wanted to keep the date they'd originally planned.

The night before she left for winter break, she gave Austin an ultimatum. He would have to agree to move the date to spring or move on without her. He chose to move on, and she was left to fall apart. My heart was heavy for my friend. I know what it's like to try to force things along, only to watch them come unhinged.

In my devotion time, the Holy Spirit reminded me how I often try to push the accelerator on promises God makes me. Just like Madison, I've been guilty of pressuring my Betrothed to make good on His promises.

The Bible describes believers as being *betrothed*, or *engaged* to Christ (2 Corinthians 11:2 NASB, where the church [the bride] will one day be joined together with Christ [the groom]).

Before Jesus left earth, He promised His disciples: "When everything is ready, I will come and get you, so that you will always be with me where I am" (John 14:3 NLT). Did you get that? The Groom lovingly promised the bride that He would come for her—"When everything is ready. I want you with me," He was saying, "but I want everything to be in order when I call you." She needed to be patient.

Love and patience go hand in hand. In fact, 1 Corinthians 13:4 defines love as "always patient" (ISV). Yet, how often do we try to move things along because we want them before they are ready?

The front wheel of my mountain bike almost rolled off once while I was racing down the road. Why? Because I had hurried the repair technician to have it put together sooner than he'd expected. And I'll admit I'm not a onetime offender. I take cinnamon rolls out of the oven half-baked. I pay double to have things shipped overnight.

I feel certain Madison and I aren't the only ones who want things when we want them. And being eager for things you've been promised isn't always a negative trait. There are good things about being eager. For example, I'm always early for meetings. My projects are turned in before their due dates. I am prepared for my assignments. I meet deadlines. I fulfill my promises when I say I will. But a positive attribute can tip the scales and work against us when we try to birth our dreams prematurely.

I believe there are things God withholds from us because of our overzealous nature to try to accomplish them apart from His strength and ahead of His time. It is our tendency to live impatiently that lures us into the trap of anxiety. The waiting process will highlight our strengths and at the same time show-case our weaknesses.

Waiting isn't something most women do well. We have become good at "passing the time" or wasting time, but few of us know how to wait well. We must become comfortable knowing that God's timing doesn't always fit our schedules. Frustration occurs the moment we put our present circumstances up against supernatural promises.

I'm sure Sarah never thought it would take ninety years for her to conceive a child. The thought of walking around *nine months along* when you're *nine decades old* is daunting. At that age most people have begun wrapping up life. Sarah was just starting life.

Earlier in this chapter I talked about God reserving the wombs of women for sovereign assignments. I want to call our attention back to that thought, because every woman has been given an assignment that no other woman can carry. There are things you can do that no one else has the skill set and calling to accomplish. We get into trouble when we start comparing the timing of what God has given us to carry with the time it takes for someone else to deliver what He has entrusted to *her*.

I remember a circle of friends who wanted to have children at the same time. They planned it out so they would be pregnant before year's end. Two of the friends conceived, but the third one could not. Watching her friends carry life when she could not was almost unbearable. What she didn't know was that the next year she would be pregnant too—with twins.

How we wait on a divine promise reveals a lot about our character. Sometimes God delays His promises, not because He doesn't want to fulfill them, but because we are not strong enough to carry them.

Let's look again at Sarah. Here's what Hebrews 11 has to

Frustration occurs the moment we put our present circumstances up against supernatural promises.

say about her: "By faith Sarah herself also *received strength* to *conceive seed,* and she bore a child when she was *past the age,* because *she judged Him faithful* who had promised (v. 11 NKJV, emphasis added).

There is so much wisdom packed into this passage. The first part of the verse reminds us that it was through faith that Sarah became strong. Most of us have physical fitness goals. We should also have spiritual fitness goals. If we are to be carriers of supernatural promises, we must grow spiritually stronger with each passing season. It's not enough for us to live off yesterday's strength. We must renew our strength daily.

The second part of the verse highlights the obvious: Sarah was past the conventional age of conception. Women her age were planning their funerals. Sarah was shopping for maternity clothes. It's not always easy moving through life at a different rhythm than our friends. Maybe, like Sarah, you had a slow start. That doesn't mean you won't wind up winning.

Don't let the frustration you are experiencing in this season of life rob you of the blessings that are in front of you. My husband and I spent seventeen months searching for a home that would meet the needs of our life and ministry. Seventeen months is a long time to hang between seasons. I admit, during those months our impatience with each other and with God's timing didn't always set a good example. It wasn't until we signed the final deed documents that I realized the home God had reserved for us hadn't even been on the market earlier. We had spent months searching for something that hadn't been built.

Have you considered that the plan God has for you is so great that He may still be carving it out? When you are tempted to just *settle*, know that God may have something in mind far greater than you've ever imagined.

> And let us not grow weary while doing good, for in due season we shall reap if we do not lose heart. (Galatians 6:9 NKJV)

> But if we hope for what we do not see, we wait eagerly for it with patience and composure. (Romans 8:25 AMP)

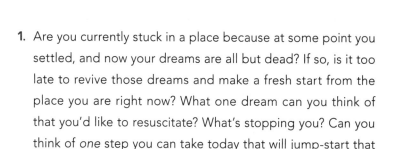

FOR Further Reflection

1. Are you currently stuck in a place because at some point you settled, and now your dreams are all but dead? If so, is it too late to revive those dreams and make a fresh start from the place you are right now? What one dream can you think of that you'd like to resuscitate? What's stopping you? Can you think of *one* step you can take today that will jump-start that forgotten dream?

2. Maybe you're not stuck in a place of "settling," but you're still not pursuing your dreams because you are afraid to. In this chapter Heather longed to open an art gallery, but her fears kept her from stepping out in faith. List the specific fears that have prevented you from stepping out in faith. Now, can you also list reasons why those fears are unfounded? Is there even a tiny move you could make today that would take you a step toward your dream?

3. In this chapter we discussed the biblical character Sarah. What we didn't discuss is the mess she made when she tried to move outside of God's timing. Read Genesis 16 and 21. Then think of a time that you made an impatient move when it would have been better to *sit still and wait*. What was the outcome? Was there fallout because of that decision to plunge ahead? If so, what have you learned from that situation?

4. Take a moment and examine your "confessions." Do you find yourself saying such things as, "No matter what I try, it never works" or, "This will never work out the way I want it to"? Perhaps you don't use these particular words, but are there other negative confessions that you tend to make, instead of speaking words of faith? What are some examples? (Here's an assignment for you, if you'd like to take this a step further: Next time you catch yourself saying negative words, write them down. Then write down an alternative, faith-filled phrase that you could say instead.)

chapter

NINE

CAPTURING YOUR COURAGE

Video surgeries make me squirm. Normally, a close-up shot of a scalpel has me groping for the remote. But today I pulled the covers close to my face and watched as a tumor was carefully removed from someone's brain.

I decided to watch the procedure after Courtney Warner shared with her online followers her diagnosis of stage 3 brain cancer. Weeks after revealing she would have a tumor extracted, she announced her decision to film the entire process . . . live. Due to the location of Courtney's tumor, the surgeons would need her to verbally communicate throughout the process. Yes. You read that right. She would have to remain awake through the entire operation. Maybe it's just me, but the thought of trying to make small talk during brain surgery unnerves me to the core.

Via YouTube, Courtney shared, "Hey guys . . . I had a pretty cool video today . . . I don't know if everyone is going to like it . . . but I think it is very interesting. A couple of weeks before my surgery I decided to film everything about the surgery. I wanted to show you how it was for me . . . beginning to end and from my perspective."

With a GoPro attached to her bed rail, Courtney is led to surgery. As the operating doors swing open, she continues to talk. "I just keep thinking, this is actually happening right now," she says.

Surgeons perform the operation while a speech therapist holds up picture flash-cards, asking Courtney to identify the images being shown. At one point the video captures a triggered seizure; the right side of Courtney's face twitches, and she is unable to communicate. She says on a later video, "I started to cry because I thought the seizure was my fault." Within a minute the seizure subsides and Courtney is once again able to identify the images. Step-by-step, Courtney courageously talks her way through the footage. The final clip ends with the subtitle, *This is when they were taking my tumor out.*[1]

As the screen faded to black, I silently asked myself, *What personal crisis would I make public if I knew it would make my sisters stronger?* Courtney's ability to turn private adversity into a shared adventure left me thinking, *Sometimes heroes don't wear capes but wear hospital gowns.*

Maybe you've never been in a situation like Courtney's, where you've had to don a hospital gown so someone can slice open your skull. But I imagine you have your own stories of times when your life spun out of control.

My friend Lauren knows the pain of watching life spin out of control. A mom of three boys—Josh, Dylan, and Ty—her life was supercharged. Between the boys' busy schedules and helping her husband, Jack, with his construction company, she watched the years slip right on by.

As she stared at the coffin, it was hard to believe twenty years had passed since first meeting Jack on a south Florida campus. It was harder to imagine that after today she would never see his face again.

What personal crisis would you make public if you knew it would make your sisters stronger?

His death was completely unexpected.

There had been no signs of heart trouble. He wasn't overweight or out of shape. No family history of coronary issues. There was no explanation for why his heart stopped. As she gently reached to touch Jack's hand, her middle son, Dylan, slipped his hand into hers. As much as she wanted to climb in the coffin with Jack, the boys needed her to claw her way back to sanity.

The months ahead were more difficult than she could have imagined. Lauren confided in me that she left off counting how many times she woke up thinking Jack was asleep beside her. She would reach for his hand only to find a pillow in his place. And she wasn't the only one grief was engulfing. Father's Day was gut-wrenching for the boys. Ty refused to eat; he simply pushed peas around his plate. Dylan missed the entire week of school, and Josh worked overtime to keep his mind distracted. Their lives were forever altered.

How do we climb out of something so deep we can't see the surface? A good place to start is on our faces in holy surrender. Sometimes surrender is the safest way to get through a season. For those of us who were born fighters, the word *surrender* has become synonymous with *defeat*. The truth is, surrender is only defeat when we hand over our authority to an equal or lesser power. Falling forward before our Father means we are surrendering but without being defeated. If there are situations that you need to surrender to God, let these words bring you comfort:

> For he will conceal me there when troubles come; he will hide me in his sanctuary. He will place me out of reach on a high rock. (Psalm 27:5 NLT)

> The LORD himself goes before you and will be with you; he will never leave you nor forsake you. Do not be afraid; do not be discouraged. (Deuteronomy 31:8 NIV)

Spending time with her Father was the first step in restoring Lauren's life. Over time and with the help of other sisters who had experienced similar pain and were willing to share their stories of restoration, her world found a new normal, and she found the strength and the courage to move on. Lauren would be the first to tell you the road to restoration wasn't without bumps or delays. There were days she felt lonely and nights that left her longing for morning. Her journey is not one any of us would want to take, but the peace she discovered in the presence of Hope Himself is something she will carry forever. Inscribed on the cover of her Bible is her life verse: "Weeping may last through the night, but joy comes with the morning" (Psalm 30:5 NLT).

If you don't have a life verse, ask God to lead you to one, and proclaim it daily. As we've discussed in previous chapters, we are made powerful by the words we proclaim. And what we hide in our hearts during secure seasons will make our hearts strong and our words sound during stormy seasons.

———

Over the years, I have tucked away countless sticky notes, manuscripts, and scrap pieces of paper. Just this week, I stumbled upon a journal shoved in the back of a moving box. Weatherworn and written in loopy letters were the words *Do all that is in your heart. Do as you wish. Behold, I am with you heart and soul.* Those words tugged at my heart. I read them over and over again: *Do as you wish . . . I am with you heart and soul.* That was the exact phrase my heart needed to read. I closed the journal and tried to remember why I had written down that phrase. Was it a quote from a play? A novel? History? A quick Google search put the phrase in context. I found the passage buried in the first book of Samuel (14:7 ESV). So, with Bible and commentary in hand, I set out to discover the significance of those words.

> What we hide in our hearts during secure seasons will make our hearts strong and our words sound during stormy seasons.

Hmm. Second year of Saul's reign. Defeat. Poverty. Trapped by enemies. Not an award-winning year for the king. Scrolling deeper, my eyes scanned for the loyal heart that had spoken those words I'd scribbled in my journal.

There they are.

Wait.

Scroll back up.

That can't be right.

An armor bearer? Not a poet? Not a prophet? But a guy carrying around a metal shield spoke these lines?

As I dug into the text, here is what I learned: With Israel's army losing ground against its enemy, there were two different schools of thought in the camp: that of the king who had run away from conflict, and that of a generation who was hungry for conquest.

Two young men—Jonathan, the king's son, and his armor bearer—decided defeat wasn't on God's agenda. So, AWOL and incognito, the pair slipped away from Saul's camp into enemy territory. They didn't ask for permission. After all, *why ask for endorsement when all you'll get is disapproval?*

Having decided to infiltrate the enemy's camp, Jonathan asked God for a sign He would be with them—and God granted it! Isn't that just like God, to give us just what we need to move forward with courage? And move forward is exactly what Jonathan did!

But what if he hadn't? What if he'd said, "Did God really *mean that?* Should I *really* move forward? What if that was just *me?* What if I'm making a big mistake?"

How many times are we guilty of asking God for permission but hesitate when He grants it? We stand at the intersection of faith and our futures, looking for a caution light when God has given us the green light.

I've discovered nothing exciting happens at a caution light. In fact, lingering at the yellow light will keep you from moving forward. Next thing you know, you've got a red light. Hesitation creates indecision, and indecision results in stagnation.

When we stick around, waiting for an audible voice from a cloud, our thoughts will begin to ramble on like this:

Wait—is it my turn, or theirs?

Were they here before or after me?

Did I just miss my opportunity to roll forward?

Do I stop or go?

Isn't that what we do? We mope around divine moments and let them slip away while we wait for signs from heaven. We find ourselves playing catch-up rather than leading with our faith. If we don't break the cycle of indecisiveness, we will miss opportunities standing before us. The bottom line is this: If we want to experience supernatural deliverance, we will have to gather our courage and confront what makes us uncomfortable, maybe even fight enemies previous generations fled from. If we are hungry for our cut of the miraculous, we will have to attempt things that place us outside our cozy comfort zones.

Jonathan had grown uncomfortable with what others were willing to tolerate.

When God gave the green light, Jonathan dropped the accelerator and steered his way forward. Dangling off the mountain, Jonathan leaned in and whispered to his companion: "Up! Follow me! GOD has turned them over to Israel!"

Jonathan scrambled up on all fours, his armor bearer right on his heels. When the Philistines came running up to them, he knocked them flat, his armor bearer right behind finishing them off, bashing their heads in with stones. In this first bloody encounter, Jonathan and his armor bearer killed about twenty men. That set off a terrific upheaval in both camp and field, the soldiers in the garrison and the raiding squad badly shaken up, the ground itself shuddering—panic like you've never seen before! (1 Samuel 14:13–15 THE MESSAGE)

Did you catch that last verse? The *earth moved*. Two men. One sword. No plan B. Sheer guts and divine impulse. No one could have predicted a boyish outing would turn into a scene from Mortal Kombat. An unauthorized but divinely sanctioned brawl would be the turning point for the army of Israel. Jonathan hadn't planned it. His armor bearer couldn't have envisioned it. But God switched on their courage, and they became victors.

There will be a time in life, if you haven't experienced it already, when God will invite you to do something daring, maybe even impulsive. How you respond to that invitation, by skulking back to your comfortable camp or running daringly forward with God, will determine whether or not you will witness a miracle. Your reaction to God's prompting will forecast your future.

Audacious faith begins with listening to the gentle whisperings of the Holy Spirit. If you want to see God perform big things, begin by obeying small instructions. Then bigger ones. Then bigger still. Soon, it will no longer be a stretch for you to follow those BIG orders from God that will result in BIG miracles, the kind you'd never counted on. When we are comfortable with doing the illogical, God can perform the unpredictable.

Harriet Ann Jacobs thought taking a swipe at the giants of her generation would be worth the risk. Harriet was born into

When we are comfortable
with doing the illogical,
God can perform the
unpredictable.

slavery in 1813, near Edenton, North Carolina. The mother of two children and only in her late teens, she was sexually harassed and threatened by her slave owner. Fearing for her life, she found the courage to flee the plantation and escaped to her grandmother's shack, where she could keep an eye on her children. For seven years she hid in the tiny crawl space of her grandmother's attic, where she could catch glimpses of her children and hear their voices.

The year the Civil War began, 1861, Jacobs's account, *Incidents in the Life of a Slave Girl, Written by Herself,* was published under the pseudonym Linda Brent. In a time when it was unusual for slaves to read and write, a firsthand account of slavery's atrocities from a woman's perspective was extraordinary. After writing her book, she continued to help those left behind in slavery. Her courage defied her critics as she helped change the political climate of a generation.[2]

It feels good to know we can write books under our own names, no matter our race. We've come a long way, fighting for personal freedoms. While I am the first to celebrate our successes, I am also aware of the battles that remain ahead of us. With great passion I tell you, *this is the season* for us to rise up and take charge of the things that have tried to crush our courage and paralyze our purpose. Nothing new will happen until we grow weary of our present condition.

Women have experienced issues in every century. One dear sister had an issue lasting well over a decade. Luke the physician wrote up her medical review this way:

In the crowd that day there was a woman who for twelve years had been afflicted with hemorrhages. She had spent every penny she had on doctors but not one had been able to help her. She slipped in from behind and touched the edge of Jesus' robe. At that very moment her hemorrhaging stopped. Jesus said, "Who touched me?"

When no one stepped forward, Peter said, "But Master, we've got crowds of people on our hands. Dozens have touched you."

Jesus insisted, "Someone touched me. I felt power discharging from me."

When the woman realized that she couldn't remain hidden, she knelt trembling before him. In front of all the people, she blurted out her story—why she touched him and how at that same moment she was healed.

Jesus said, "Daughter, you took a risk trusting me, and now you're healed and whole. Live well, live blessed!" (Luke 8:43–48 THE MESSAGE)

Have you ever felt like falling at Jesus' feet and blurting out your story? Every time I read this sister's tale, I want to stand up and shout, "I've got issues too!" It took a lot of moxie to crawl out of the corner and put her drama out in the daylight. I'm amazed she was brave enough to tell her story and then wait around for Jesus' reaction. I would have rambled through my tale and run off so I wouldn't see the expression on His face.

In my own prayer times, I've been known to blurt out things bothering me, hoping I didn't make God blush. I've asked Him for miracles while crossing my fingers in hopes that He wouldn't bring up my mistakes. I've talked about my dreams and droned on about my doubts. I'm sure I haven't been the easiest daughter to deal with. Maybe in some ways we are all a little challenging—we have "issues." But here is the beautiful thing: *In all of our time together, I've never had my Father get up and walk out of the room.* Not one time. He stays around until my issues are resolved.

Our Father doesn't just respond to daughters who have it all together. His grace reaches to those of us who only have strength to fall at His feet. With empathy, He listens as we blurt out things we don't want others to hear. Sticky issues that would make our friends squirm. Awkward topics many would find inappropriate. He doesn't care that you bring messes to the meeting. He loves that you have the courage to face Him and to trust Him to mend your messes.

There is no one who cares more about your healing than your Father. His eyes are upon you, and His ears listen for your faintest cry. Our meeting with Him isn't to prove our strength, but to discover His.

Hurt influences our dreams in ways our heroes cannot. When I think of sheroes, my friend Bonnie Floyd immediately comes to mind. In *Bound to a Promise*, she shares how personal devastation, including murder and betrayal, headline her story of redemption.

If you ever have the chance to meet Bonnie, you'll be amazed by her fearless determination to turn tragedy into a treasure hunt for truth. It's not every day I find someone with enough faith to turn tragedy into triumph. Bonnie did. Her quest to reach the very nation that took her family from her is a script destined for the big screen. But those kinds of super-natural assignments aren't given to the superficial. They are entrusted to sheroes who take a sideswipe from injustice and are willing to allow the brutal to be transformed into something beautiful.

How we handle our hurts has much to do with how our destiny unfolds. Destiny is not a place. It is a decision we make, often after life has hurled injustice our way. Most everyone wants a supernatural testimony of faith, but few are willing to sacrifice their fears on the altar of faith to have one. We desire the celebration story as long as it isn't painful. Most of the time, when life gets sticky, we look for the easy way out. Here's the hard truth:

If you're looking for the easy way out, you'll discover it.
If you're searching for a quick fix, you'll find one.
If you pursue wisdom, you'll possess it.
If you chase down your dreams, you'll achieve them.

God-sized dreams aren't for the fragile and faint of heart. I've yet to see a miracle moment that wasn't messy. When God looks to do something grand in our lives, it usually feels more like we're in a war zone than a comfort zone. There are only a handful of Bible stories that would qualify for a G rating. The best of God's men and women lived edgy, complicated lives. It was their faith that God would transform their stories into something glorious that kept them on this side of sanity.

When my heart is heavy with grief or burdened in some way, I open my Bible to the book of Psalms. Today, if you are walking through a difficult season, I encourage you to commit these words to memory.

> When the LORD restored the fortunes of Zion,
>> we were like those who dream.
> Then our mouth was filled with laughter,
>> and our tongue with shouts of joy;
> then they said among the nations,
>> "The LORD has done great things for them."
> The LORD has done great things for us;
>> we are glad.
>
> (Psalm 126:1–3 ESV)

There is no superscription naming the writer who inscribed these words. No date. No time stamp. No trademark. But there is a common belief among scholars that Ezra wrote these words the day the Jews were released from Babylon. I've tried to imagine what it was like the first time they walked beyond the gates of captivity. I feel certain that tears of joy fell from the cheeks of burly men. Mothers imagined their children dancing in the streets of Jerusalem. Fathers envisioned hammering together their homes in early spring. The moment was spectacular, like a dream to those who experienced it.

I've experienced similar miracles. It is an overwhelming feeling to have your dream realized unexpectedly. Suddenly, what *can be* becomes what *shall be*. It is one thing to imagine dancing in the streets; it's another to feel the gravel crunch beneath your toes.

Before we move forward I want us to look back over this passage one more time. Go with me to the first line, find the word *restored*, and underline it. Then take your highlighter if you have one, and mark the words *laughter*, *joy*, and *glad*. Now push your pen from the word *restored* to the words I had you highlight. See the correlation? When restoration comes, it brings gladness with it. God longs to heal the areas that have robbed us of our peace. He wants us to gather our courage following times of adversity and move forward.

As I close this chapter, I want us to pray this prayer together.

Dear Father,

You did not create your daughters to walk around timid or afraid. But You placed within each of us the heart of a warrior. We acknowledge that You have not given us the spirit of fear, but of power, love, and a sound mind. According to that promise, we step out of the shadows of apprehension and shame and into the light of Your grace. As we walk in Your truth, we shake free from strongholds of doubt and discouragement and recapture the courage to do bold, new things. We embrace what You have set aside for us, knowing we hold a special place in Your heart. In total confidence and freedom, we move forward with the assignment You have given us. Grant us favor, wisdom, and courage.

FOR

Further Reflection

1. When Lauren lost her husband, she was surrounded by sisters who had walked in her shoes, and they supported her through that dark time. Are you going through a dark time such as Lauren's? If so, who could you turn to for the kind of support she received? On the other hand, to whom could you give support who is facing a dark time that you have already gone through and conquered?

2. Have you ever asked God for a sign or for direction and then questioned it when it came? What kind of confirmation were you seeking? Did you act on it, or did you flip-flop back and forth between decision and indecision?

3. In this chapter we looked at the concept of *surrendering*. Are you in a situation right now about which you can do nothing *but* surrender it—and yourself—to the Lord? Are you tempted to take matters into your own hands and force a solution? Or are you willing to get in God's presence, surrender the problem to Him, and let Him take the wheel?

4. In this chapter we read about the hemorrhaging woman who had suffered with her issue for twelve years. By that time, many of us would have long lost our hope and given up. Is there a long-term issue you've been dealing with that has worn you down to the point of giving up? Remember that all it took was one moment in the presence of Jesus to turn our Bible friend's whole life around. Might your miracle be just one touch away?

chapter
TEN

GOD'S SILENCE, OUR WORDS

Entwined in the historical exploits of famed explorers Lewis and Clark, you will stumble upon an unsuspecting hero. Born to a Shoshone chief, Sacagawea was kidnapped by an enemy tribe at age twelve and sold to a French-Canadian trapper.

Let's stop right there. Sitting in our comfortable homes, it is difficult to imagine the horror of being kidnapped by an invading native tribe. But what if, instead of a tribe, the enemy was a rival gang. Suppose an SUV full of gangbangers rolled up and grabbed your twelve-year-old daughter. The thought brings to surface every parent's primal fear. Taken. Sold. Trafficked. Pregnant.[1]

Finding yourself captive, submerged in a culture where no one speaks your language, isn't on anyone's to-do list. It's on the *never-do* list. But choosing to make the best of a horrifying situation is the story line that takes ordinary people out of the ranks of average and records their names in the historical list of who's who.

Reference books don't document Sacagawea's struggles during her early years of captivity. All we know is a young pregnant girl used her gift of language interpretation and knowledge of botany to assist Lewis and Clark on their expedition to the Pacific. Of the daring group of thirty-three elite explorers, Sacagawea was the only woman to make the voyage. A valued interpreter between rival tribes, she became a symbol of peace in war-torn regions. Not only did she transform gut-wrenching circumstances into a positive life experience, her son born during the cross-country expedition became the famed explorer Jean Baptiste. A challenge that would have destroyed others became a crosspoint with destiny.

Facing our challenges does not feel good. Fighting for custodial care of your children isn't easy. Posting bail for your son's DUI turns your stomach inside out. Waving goodbye to thirty years of job security to launch a startup company takes courage. Waging a campaign against sex trafficking lands you far from your comfort zone.

So, how do we respond when life calls on us to act in a way that sets our faith on a collision course with our fears? Do we run for cover at the first signs of conflict? Do we slip out of our superhero capes and into fluffy footie pajamas? Or, like Sacagawea, do we dig down deep and find a way to turn a nightmare into something meaningful?

This fall, at a convention, I enjoyed lunch with a colleague. Warmhearted and caring, she is someone I greatly admire. Her family heads up a nonprofit corporation providing clean water and clothing to families in economically depressed areas. Both the family and corporation have a reputation for being honest and generous. That is why my face went pale when she began to tell me about a handful of *big-name believers* who had bad-mouthed their organization. I wanted to tell her their words didn't carry weight, but I knew they did.

I hope you've never had your good works slandered. More than likely you have, probably more than once. It's not easy when evil people fire shots at your labor of love. But it is almost unbearable when you are blindsided by people who should be supporting your cause.

There is no pass that can prevent us from having to deal with those who only want to talk well of themselves. But we can take charge of how we respond when arrows from our tribe are pointed at our hearts. For years, I let mudslinging pull my attention away from my purpose. Now that I have developed a closer walk with my Father and understand how enemies can work in my favor, I celebrate when clouds of persecution begin to gather on the horizon. Rather than trying to protect my heart, I actually run toward challenges. That may sound like a Pollyannaish approach. But as a daughter who is confident her Father works all things together for her good, I know hidden within the clouds of pain is a rainbow of promise. It's comforting to know that even when we must walk through seasons of suffering, we will run straight into God's promises. Tying His promises to our hearts will keep our emotions from unraveling.

I wasn't always so mature in my response to adversity. There were times I wanted God to step in and say something about how I was being treated. It seemed the more I prayed for a word from God, the more silent He became on the subject. What I didn't realize is that just because God doesn't speak, it doesn't mean He doesn't see or that He won't respond or that He's not moving in our situation. His eyes are always on His daughters. And He's always fighting on our behalf.

> The LORD *looks* down from heaven
>> and *sees* every person.
> From his throne he *watches*
>> all who live on earth.
> He made their hearts
>> and understands everything they do. . . .
> But the LORD *looks after* those who fear him,
>> those who put their hope in his love.
>>> (Psalm 33:13–15, 18, emphasis added)

The LORD will fight for you while you [only need to] keep silent and remain calm. (Exodus 14:14 AMP)

Maybe you have wondered where God is in your situation. Not in an accusing kind of way, but in a "Why-haven't-you-shown-up-yet?" kind of way. It could be our Father wants us to find comfort in His *presence*, not just in His *voice*.

Sometimes when I am going through deep trials, just having a friend show up and sit beside me brings comfort. She doesn't have to bring words of wisdom to the table; her presence speaks volumes about her loyalty. This could be true of our Father. We don't have to *hear* His voice in order to feel His presence.

He doesn't always pull up a chair beside you because He has something to say. Sometimes His presence is His way of showing you, *I'm on your side.*

In our longing for words, we may be missing something greater—the warmth of His presence. We must learn to listen to what He is saying when He is saying nothing at all.

If we can't understand God's silence, how will we ever make sense of His words?

Over time I have discovered that our Father doesn't always step into our situations with words but sometimes with signs and wonders. God controls our destinies in ways we may never consider.

I get emotional when I read the story of Joseph. I can't help it. When I think of the unnecessary heartache he went through, a sigh of empathy escapes my lips. If you've been pushed into dark places by people you love, you understand the pain I'm referring to. Sometimes the heaviest sorrows we carry were placed on us by people we love most.

> We must learn to listen to what He is saying when He is saying nothing at all.

There have been many moments in life when I seriously questioned if there was anything redeemable about the season I was walking through. I'm sure some of you have felt the same way. Maybe you feel that way now. By the heaviness I feel as I write these words, I am confident someone is clawing her way through a situation that has robbed her of her peace. As a sister, I caution you to steer away from the temptation to run for cover and hide during this trying time. Isolation isn't our friend. If anything, isolation slowly steals our identity.

I know it's easy to cower from things that require confrontation. But if we can learn to walk through trials with our identity intact, we will position ourselves for promotion.

When Joseph's brothers threw him in a pit, God seemed strangely silent. No thunderous voice from heaven. No angelic visitation. No divine intervention. During one of the darkest seasons of life, the only people who showed up for Joseph were a band of slave traders.

Those who thought they were purchasing a slave were positioning the prince of Egypt.

Years later, when Joseph was falsely imprisoned, the heavens were once again eerily silent. There were no inspiring words for the innocent. No heavenly mediation that would make the situation hopeful. *Sometimes silence screams.*

As I retraced Joseph's journey, I can't tell you his story was laced together with prophetic words. I've learned prophecies aren't always put on paper. What I did discover was something deeper, more comforting than words. *God didn't speak to Joseph, He showered him with favor.*

Not every love language comes wrapped as a verbal package. Sometime actions do speak louder than words. God told Joseph . . .

I see you.
I hear you.
I love you.
I haven't forsaken you.
I still have a grand purpose for your life.

. . . in ways that weren't so obvious:

The LORD was with Joseph, so he succeeded in everything he did as he served in the home of his Egyptian master. (Genesis 39:2 NLT)

But the LORD was with Joseph in the prison and showed him his faithful love. And the LORD made Joseph a favorite with the prison warden. (Genesis 39:21 NLT)

Divine favor defended Joseph in a way that didn't require God to say a word. In fact, every breakthrough in Joseph's journey came through the hands of his enemies. God never defended Joseph with talk but with action; He used his enemies to advance His son.

Joseph was destined to rule Egypt. Each time his enemies tried to harm him they positioned him closer to the palace.

His brothers threw him in a pit—it would move him closer to Egypt.

Midianite slave traders bought Joseph as a slave—and carried him to Egypt.

Potiphar's wife falsely accused Joseph—and he was placed in prison next to the palace.

The king's cupbearer remembered that he could interpret dreams—and brought him before the king.

Today, no matter how far off course you think you are, you may be exactly where God wants you. He may not be making a sound, but He's working on your promotion—He may even use your enemies as the catalysts!

In my quiet time with the Lord, He gave me these words. I scribbled them in my journal as a reminder of God's faithfulness. I hope they will be an encouragement to you, especially if you are discouraged with the silence of God:

There is a season coming when you will receive great increase from those who once despised you. As you break free from the chains that have kept you back, blurred your focus, and sold you the lie that you are not good enough, God will restore your wealth, health, and vision.

When Israel left for the promised land, they walked out in battle formation with the riches of Egypt on their backs. God will perform His word in a day. Believe it.

The LORD said to Moses, "I have made you like God to the king of Egypt, and your brother Aaron will be like a prophet for you. . . . But I will make the king stubborn. I will do many miracles in Egypt, but he will still refuse to listen. So then I will punish Egypt . . . with my power, and I will bring the Israelites out of that land. Then they will know I am the LORD." (Exodus 7:1–6)

It's never easy being the voice of reason, especially when you are sent to talk to the unreasonable. If God has ever asked you to share His Word with someone you haven't seen in a few decades, you might have an appreciation for what Moses was going through. It had been four decades since Moses had seen Pharaoh. No postcard. No email. No family gathering. It was an awkward kind of reunion, the kind you hope you're never forced to attend.

Moses didn't show up at the palace because he was lonely. He showed up because he had been sent with something to say. Many times we push away from how God wants to use us because we dread the feeling that comes with confronting what is familiar. Pharaoh wasn't just *familiar* with Moses, he was Moses' adoptive grandfather. I've learned that prophetic words aren't always for those we don't know; sometimes they are for the ones we know *well*.

I wish I could tell you that following God always feels good. But I don't want to mislead you. Sometimes God will ask us to do things that make us feel more fragile than fearless. Getting on board with God's plan isn't always comfortable. In fact, the feeling can be similar to wearing a wool sweater in summer. I'm certain that's how Moses felt when he delivered words of *doom* to Pharaoh—*uncomfortable*, in an itchy-sweater kind of way. After all, Moses hadn't picked a fight with Pharaoh; God had. Moses was simply acting as God's ambassador.

There are times God will ask us to speak words that are more confrontational than comforting. I've spent many sleepless nights trying to weigh out words God wanted me to speak. It's not so risky when God asks us to speak in front of strangers, but what about when He asks us to talk plainly to our tribe?

I remember a conference where I was invited to speak when I was in my early thirties. I can recall the exact message God placed in my heart to deliver. My fear wasn't that I hadn't heard from God; I feared I had. The conference had a reputation for hosting high-energy speakers who spoke positive types of messages. I'm not downing upbeat messages; I have a stockpile of them. But that weekend I felt more like Moses than Madea. The word God had given me made the conference hall feel less like Disneyland and more like a delivery room.

Speaking up in sticky situations is something we as women have to get better at doing. We can't blow the opportunity for our voices to be amplified just as our gender is getting comfortable with having our voices heard.

Sometimes God will

ask us to do things

that make us feel more

fragile than fearless.

For decades men and women have been classified as being from different planets. This adage hits the mark when it comes to how men and women use social media. Marketing companies reveal that men use social media primarily for business purposes while women capitalize on the networking perks. After years of following our social footprints, media trackers discovered women are more vocal and more expressive, and they reveal more about their personal lives than men. On average, women have more than twice as many posts on social sites, and they have 8 percent more "friends" than men. In other words, they confirmed what we've always known: women are biologically wired for networking.

When I swipe through my media feed, it is obvious our gender looks at the world through a different lens than men do. By *different* I don't mean in a divisive kind of way. But different in how we approach life and the priorities we hold close to our hearts. Many nights my husband and I curl up on our couch and scan our social sites, and the posts he finds interesting or funny I let slide right past. Things that draw me in often turn him away. That is because men and women are wired to interact differently.

The other night my husband read the post of a lady I've met for coffee a few times. Too polite to say anything negative about what she had written, he gave me the look men have when they think someone is being dramatic. In return I gave him a *Don't mess with her; we are part of the same tribe* look.

As I've studied the writings of my sisters, I have found that we crave social interaction because we want to be accepted, understood, and empowered. We want to be accepted as we *are*, understood for what we are *going through*, and empowered for the *journey* in front of us. We also have a heart for helping others, and we are the most emotionally healthy when we are sowing into one another the things we desire most. Our words are often our way of doing that, and they are more powerful than we've ever imagined. But living in a social media–driven society, we also allow our thoughts and opinions on delicate issues to spill over into the lives of people we will never meet.

A dear sister with a large media platform accidentally let her own wounds bleed through her words. When a hot, controversial topic hit the fan, she fired off a round of tweets before taking time to weigh out her words. Trust me when I tell you, she wasn't gentle. These tweets were of the flame-throwing, name-calling, how-dare-you kind. From the way she engaged, it was clear the topic had touched a sore spot where she had yet to receive healing. But worse, this sister then faced a flood of negative backlash from her followers. Once considered a champion for social issues, she was now viewed as a bully due to her careless and even caustic remarks.

Sometimes our wounds show up in the worst kind of settings.

Of course, I've created my own share of messes. This last year, I found myself tangled up in a war of words over a petty issue. I will spare you the details of the story. Suffice it to say, someone picked a fight, and I picked up my sword.

When someone picks a fight, don't always reach for your sword.

I don't like making mistakes. In fact, messing up leaves me in a miserable mood. I'll be the first to tell you I'm still learning how to capture my thoughts and refine them before releasing them. After absorbing a few punches for how I've worded things, I've made progress by choosing to let my thoughts linger in my head before ever allowing them to fall from my lips. If we are to lead our culture in truth, we are not only responsible for *what* we say, but for *how* and *where* we say it.

Not long ago, a friend called to tell me she was feeling lonely and left out. Through social media, she'd discovered two of her friends had moved forward with a dream the three of them once shared. She went on to explain that, months earlier, while on vacation, the friends had spent time planning a start-up company in the travel industry—a company they were to run together. Now seeing that the other two had started their venture without her left her with a crushed heart.

After she finished sharing her story, I used the remainder of the call to ramble on about how disloyal people can be, even those we consider to be trusted friends. I passed along stories I'd heard from other people and firsthand stories of my own. A good twenty minutes passed before I heard soft cries on the other end of the call. I finally quit talking and realized how far off the mark my words had fallen. In an effort to defend my friend, I had overlooked the obvious: she didn't need the words of a warrior; she needed the warmth of a woman with a listening ear. And if I were going to say anything at all, it should have been words of empathy and healing, not a diatribe against those who had hurt me. Since that conversation, I've learned to pray for wisdom before plunging into someone's pain, so I'll know whether to listen or to speak. If I do speak, I will be more diligent to speak words of life and healing rather than letting my words run wild.

Here are a few scriptures that remind us to keep careful watch over our words. Meditate on them, as they may help you to not make the same mistakes I have.

Let your speech at all times be gracious *and* pleasant, seasoned with salt, so that you will know how to answer each one [who questions you]. (Colossians 4:6 AMP)

Careless words stab like a sword,
    but wise words bring healing.
(Proverbs 12:18)

A gentle answer will calm a person's anger,
    but an unkind answer will cause more anger.
(Proverbs 15:1)

A soothing tongue [speaking words that build up
    and encourage] is a tree of life,
But a perversive tongue [speaking words that
    overwhelm and depress] crushes the spirit.
(Proverbs 15:4 AMP)

January in Tanzania, Africa, meant one thing: rain. Not a soft drizzle either, but a downpour. Two weeks of meetings were drawing to a close, and the night before our departure, we were scheduled to attend the wedding of an African dignitary.

Dressed in our wedding garments, we were escorted to the section reserved for the bridal party. The night was festive, an evening devoted to culture and cuisine. As the celebration drew to a close, the father of the bride asked me to release a prophetic word over his daughter. He explained it was customary for an older married woman to speak words of wisdom to the bride. I must confess, I didn't like the thought of being labeled *older*, and I staggered at the thought of speaking words to a bride I'd only met days earlier. I started to refuse his offer, but with thousands of attendees staring, I felt it would be offensive for me to say no. Forcing a smile, I nervously walked to the platform and waited for someone to translate English into Swahili. Silently I said a prayer. *Lord, give me words that will speak to the soul of this bride.* Although I cannot recall the entire prayer blessing, there are parts that still linger in my heart.

Here is a part of the blessing that welled out of my mouth much like the rainstorm poured out of the sky hours before:

> *May you, Ashanti, have the . . .*
> *courage of Esther to walk with royalty,*
> *prophetic insights of Deborah to guide your nation,*
> *grace of Sarah to conceive divine promises,*
> *favor of Ruth,*
> *purity of Mary,*
> *and a legacy that rises up and calls you "blessed one."*

With all the mistakes I've made when I've opened my mouth, this was one time when I used my mouth to bless. I hope this chapter has taught you to bless your sisters with your words, and as I close this chapter, I hope you will embrace the blessing above for yourself. Because those words aren't just for a tribal princess, but for every woman who is a daughter of the King.

1. Have you, like Sacagawea or Joseph, ever spent considerable time in a situation in which you felt trapped, only to discover that in the end, God really does make all things beautiful in His time? What was that adverse situation? What blessings did God bring out of that situation? If you are still in such a situation, do these two stories give you hope for a happy ending?

2. When has God defended you in a situation, even as He remained silent? Though you weren't hearing from Him, did His presence alone bring you great comfort? In what ways did He come to your defense in the midst of His silence?

3. Think of a time when someone came against you and it only resulted in things working out for your good. Did God use your enemies to promote you? What was the nature of their attack? What was the outcome?

4. Reflect on your social media posts. Do you tend to use social media to share your life's events, your family photos, and your witticisms, or do you tend to use it as a platform for taking aim at people and their issues? How can you be more prudent when using social media? Do you take the time to think (and pray) before you post?

chapter
ELEVEN

STORMY SEASONS

Waves lapped over the edge of the boat. My deck shoes filled with salt water. It was my second time sailing, and storm clouds were forming.

As the boat began to pitch and turn, I asked the captain of the vessel how I could help us get away from the storm. Yelling above the wind, he said something that still lingers with me: "Don't try to get away from something you can't outrun!" Squinting and shaking my head, I yelled back, "But I came here to learn to sail!" He dropped the line and placed his hands on his hips. "You won't learn by sailing when the sea is calm. Take advantage of the storm that is coming. Learn to lean into the wind."

Learning to lean into stormy situations was not an achievement I mastered in a single session. Like every great lesson in life, it took a few rounds of being dumped on my backside before I found my sea legs. I wanted to walk like a sailor, not wobble like a penguin. It took some time and practice before I could move about on steady legs in any weather.

Isn't that just like all of life? Learning how to steady ourselves and walk comfortably when everything around us is shaky takes practice.

There is a part of us that wants to activate our faith, but without looking foolish. Our pride fights to keep us from pursuing anything that would make us appear imperfect. I could have just quit sailing to avoid the embarrassment. But I stuck it out.

I wish I could give you illustrations of how I've walked in faith without drawing attention to my flaws and insecurities. I can't. I've yet to do something memorable without making some type of mistake. But that's the way it is. A brave life almost guarantees you will make some kind of blunder or experience some level of uncertainty. And if you desire miracles to be a part of your life script, then doubt, fear, and anxiety are also guaranteed to show up without invitation. The uncomfortable feeling of doing something daring can be a sign of weakness, but it can also be the catalyst that gives you the strength to survive the storm.

Though God's Word doesn't guarantee that every situation will be peaceful, it does guarantee that if we live for Christ, we can have peace in every situation and through any storm.

I cannot remember a single miracle that had a serene backdrop. Think about that for a moment. Every biblical miracle I've read about came in the midst of some kind of storm.

- Jesus restored an amputated ear in the midst of His own betrayal and arrest.
- Jesus healed a lame man even as His enemies challenged and accused Him.

- Jesus cast out demons from a hopelessly insane—and naked—man.
- Jesus raised a decomposing man to life in spite of unbelief and even a plot to take His life.

And that's only the beginning of the miracles Jesus performed in the midst of a storm. He calmed the storms in people's lives: extortionists, beggars, lepers, divorcees, and even the blind. Not one of His miracles came in the midst of a peaceful situation but a chaotic one. And storms leave messes in their wake. Maybe that is something we need to consider when we find ourselves shying away from taking part in others' miracles. Miracles are not designed for the comfortable and composed but for the troubled and tortured. It's a stormy business. When we sign up to take part in others' miracles, we need to bring both our faith and a mop for swabbing the deck.

Some storms are not so hard to make it through with your faith intact. But then there are those others. The ones where the winds are strong and they're hitting you from every direction. I can relate . . .

My husband and I were in the middle of an IRS audit. Our car was totaled by a hit-and-run driver. We were having a hard time with one of our children. A neighbor had threatened to file a frivolous lawsuit. A close friend and board member unexpectedly passed away. Everything was going wrong. Nothing was going right. At least that's how it felt.

With all the chaos that went on that summer, our circumstances could have shaken our faith in our God. We could have capsized. Been thrown overboard. But instead, we resolved to spend our summer preaching on faith—on purpose. We were determined to make declarations that would breathe life into our faith and suffocate our fears during that most dreadful storm. And that's exactly what we did. We preached faith, and as summer began to fade, so did our fears.

One Wednesday night in August, after my husband, Robby, finished preaching, a man approached him and handed him a wrinkled envelope. Assuming it was a note or Scripture verse, Robby thanked him and tucked the envelope in his jacket pocket. Hours later, when he took off his jacket, the envelope fell out and onto the bed. Curious, he slid open the flap. Inside was a check for fifty thousand dollars. Looking back, I can almost feel that storm cease as the hurricane-force winds evaporated into a balmy breeze. That's what happens when you trust your Father.

Sometimes a storm takes its sweet time brewing. Slowly, slowly, the storm clouds form and there's ample time to take cover. But other times, those storm clouds arise—and collide—without warning. How do we prepare for them? How do we survive them?

On a road trip recently, my friend shared an amazing story. The week before Hurricane Katrina, she and her husband had called their church together for a time of prayer and fasting. They had no idea how significant those days of intercession would become. Overnight the streets of their city turned into rivers. Cell phone towers were down, and families were separated from each other. They spent months trying to locate the members of their church. One by one they tracked them down, and each family had an extraordinary testimony to share of God's faithfulness. One man had this story to tell:

During the height of the storm, I lost my footing and was unexpectedly swept away by the flood. Alone in the dark, I fought to keep my head above the water's current. Panicking, I began searching for something I could use to float on until help arrived. I reached for what appeared to be a giant wooden door and climbed on top. Three days later, a helicopter arrived and pulled me out of the water.

It was then I discovered what I had been floating on was not a door but an upside-down casket. A thing that had been created to carry death was the only thing keeping me alive.

The moral of that story is this: God will see you through your storm—and He'll use anything at His disposal to do it . . . even a casket!

But there's more. God has the ability to turn our stormy seasons into balmy, beautiful seasons in life. With incredible awe I have watched God turn terrible storms into something beautiful. Maybe that is what you need today. A spectacular ending to something that once promised only tragedy. Our enemy seeks to destroy us in the storm. But God stays by our sides, protecting us and guiding us through it until storm clouds pass over.

I don't say these words out of my own imagination but out of experience. It would take days of us sitting together to share all the miracle moments I've witnessed over the years that started in the midst of a horrendous storm. I've watched mothers pray their sons out of prison. Daughters miraculously healed of cancer. Drug addicts walk away from their dealers. There is nothing God would rather do than turn your storm clouds into peaceful moments and your heartache into hope.

Often, it is during the storms of life that we learn some of the most valuable lessons. In the stormiest time of one woman's life, she learned that sometimes the only solution is to *let go.*

Indeed, some of our most miraculous moments occur when God asks us to release the things we hold closest to our hearts. If we're willing to do it, it's amazing what God can do. That's what Jochebed learned in the midst of the biggest storm she would ever face. Here's how it went down.

The Hebrews were slaves to Pharaoh, the king of Egypt. But blessed by God, these slaves were becoming a threat to Egypt—at least that's how he saw it. They were beginning to outnumber the Egyptians.

So Pharaoh gave this order to the midwives: "Watch the Hebrew women as they give birth. If they deliver a baby girl, fine. But if the baby is a boy . . . kill him!"

But the midwives feared God, and they refused to obey the king's orders. They allowed the baby boys to live. When the king learned that the midwives had disobeyed him, he demanded to know why they had not killed the infant boys.

"Hebrew women are not Egyptian women," the midwives lied. "They are much more vigorous. By the time we get there to help them deliver, their babies have already been born!"

So the Hebrews continued to multiply, growing more

and more powerful—and more of a threat to the threatened Pharaoh. Wicked old Pharaoh. As if his first mandate weren't bad enough, he came up with another one, even more sinister than the first: "Throw every newborn Hebrew boy into the Nile River" (Exodus 1:1–22, paraphrased).

I don't think any of us would like to live in a culture where a king can decide what becomes of our unborn babies. But that's precisely the culture in which Jochebed found herself. Fearing that a ruler would rise to power from among the sons of Israel, the king had issued a death decree over the sons of Israel.

How can you possibly protect what you cannot defend? Jochebed felt powerless. In such an environment, she would have had to hide her pregnancy. If she was successful to that point, then she would have to hide her son. To save her son's life would be to risk her own.

I see some parallels here to our lives today. We, like Jochebed, have an enemy too. He may not be gunning for our babies, but he is surely gunning for our dreams. Like Pharaoh, our enemy senses when we have conceived something that can do great damage to his kingdom. He wants to terminate it. Don't be surprised if things get dark right before you're ready to deliver your dream.

Right before launching our first television program, we faced a wave of dark threats against our family. These were not just the grumblings of someone who didn't want us to succeed. It was an all-out conspiracy. Our dream was in danger. Have you been there? Have you ever felt that the dream you were carrying was in danger of being terminated?

Sometimes we have to keep our dreams to ourselves until it's time to deliver. A prophetic promise will need to be tucked away in our hearts, hidden away from those who could do it harm, until the day when God is ready to bring it to fruition. I've learned to pay attention when I feel a check about sharing with someone what is growing on the inside of me. You must do the same.

Warnings can come in the form of divine nudges. I learned that when, excited to share something God was doing through our ministry outreaches, I started to let the news slide across my lips. Halfway through the announcement, I felt the Holy Spirit nudge me to stop talking. Shutting down my statement midsentence left me feeling awkward. A few months later, though, I discovered that someone I had thought was safe had turned out to be unstable. Had I shared my heart with that person, it could have meant the end of my dream. I've since learned that the same maternal instinct that God has given us to protect our unborn children has also been given us to quietly carry our unborn dreams.

Jochebed did give birth to her child, and for as long as she was able, she hid him in her home, doing her best to cover up his cries and hide the evidence of having a newborn in the house.

"But when she could no longer hide him," we are told, "she got a basket made of papyrus reeds and waterproofed it with tar and pitch." And then, desperate to protect her child and not let him be stripped away from her, "she put the baby in the basket and laid it among the reeds along the bank of the Nile River" (Exodus 2:3 NLT). *She let it go.*

Imagine placing your infant son in a basket in a crocodile-infested river. Watching that basket drift slowly out of sight. Releasing your child out of your care and into God's. And hoping against hope that God *will* take care of him—or at least send him to someone who will.

It's never easy to release the things we love. Especially when we've conceived and carried them.

Jochebed must have spent many sleepless nights questioning:

Do I press on trying to protect my child, or do I let his fate fall into the hands of his heavenly Father?

Will my son be safer in my house or in God's hands?

Do I trust God enough to place back in His arms what He all too briefly let me hold in mine?

I wonder if your faith has been tested in a similar way. It's never easy to release the things we've been entrusted to love. Over the years, God has asked me to release loved ones, dreams, and friends I wasn't ready to let go of. But I can tell you that it's easier on the heart to hand over those things we hold dear than to have them pried out of our hands.

It took awhile for me to realize it, but I've discovered that God never shortchanges His daughters. He will only ask you to release something in this season if He knows there is something better in the season to come. And something supernatural happens when we release what is in our nature to protect.

Follow me back into this story for one last look:

[Jochebed] put the basket among the tall stalks of grass at the edge of the Nile River. The baby's sister stood a short distance away to see what would happen to him. Then the daughter of the king of Egypt came to the river to take a bath, and her servant girls were walking beside the river. When she saw the basket in the tall grass, she sent her slave girl to get it. The king's daughter opened the basket and saw the baby boy. He was crying, so she felt sorry for him and said, "This is one of the Hebrew babies."

Then the baby's sister asked the king's daughter, "Would you like me to go and find a Hebrew woman to nurse the baby for you?" The king's daughter said, "Go!"

So the girl went and got the baby's own mother. The king's daughter said to the woman, "Take this baby and nurse him for me, and I will pay you." So the woman took her baby and nursed him. When the child grew older, the woman took him to the king's daughter, and she adopted the baby as her own son. The king's daughter named him Moses, because she had pulled him out of the water. (Exodus 2:3–10)

What we are willing to release into God's hands, He can use to bring miracles to our lives. Jochebed released her son to God—and God released a nation through her son. Her infant Moses, placed in God's hands, would one day become her deliverer.

Now, are you holding on tight to something—or someone—that needs to be *let go*? If so, recall that every good thing we have is only given to us on loan from the Father. He gives them to us to watch over, or for a time. When that time is up, we have to be willing to let them go. Those bad things, the ones He *didn't* send our way, we also have to be willing to let *them* go. In either case, our responsibility is to trust God and *let go*. If it's a dream that you're clutching, but God wants you to let it go, remember that God loves you, and He has a better dream. It may even involve your original dream. He put it there in the first place, you know. Case in point: Jochebed wanted a baby. God gave her a deliverer. And both baby *and* deliverer were her son.

God never shortchanges His daughters.

I cannot tell you what would have become of Moses if his mother had continued trying to keep him hidden. Perhaps both she and her son would have died. But what I do know is that almost three million slaves walked out of captivity because one woman yielded to what later was seen to be a plan ordained by God. This book is all about bravery, and it takes great bravery to yield. And it takes bravery to *let go*.

When her infant son returned to Egypt as her deliverer, you can bet Jochebed was there to see him. The stormiest season of her life was long forgotten. God had led her through the storm—and led the *entire nation* of Israel to freedom.

And all because she was willing to *let go*.

May God give us the wisdom to know what to hold on to and what to let go—and the courage to release what needs to fly free.

My cell phone buzzed late one night. I started not to answer, but when I saw the call was from Emma I decided to take it. Sleepily I said, "Hello." From the other end of the call came soft sobs and broken words. My heart sank and I braced myself for words I didn't want to hear.

"Em, talk to me, honey, are you okay?" For a long moment I heard nothing.

Then between sobs came the words, "I . . . don't . . . know."

I tried to stay calm and not imagine the worst-case scenario. "What do you mean by *you don't know?* Are you not feeling well? Are you having contractions? Has your water broken? Tell me what's going on." Another long pause.

"Well, I haven't felt Lily move around today. She's not kicking. Everything feels . . . still."

I tried to think of something positive to say. "How many weeks along are you?"

She quickly said, "Thirty-seven weeks."

My mind raced, searching for a memory to pull from. It took me a moment, but then I remembered something important. "Oh, honey, I think you are going to be fine. A few weeks before my due date, my daughter quit moving too. It wasn't because anything was wrong. She was simply getting into the birthing position."

"Really, that happened to you too?"

I could almost hear her smiling through the phone. Emma and I continued to talk for the next half hour. A text came through late the next day saying, "Things are looking good. I felt little Lily kick."

It took a long time for me to let loose of that conversation. I began to think about how we as women have been designed to carry life. I'm not just referring to how we carry our children but our dreams as well. Much like my friend Emma, some of you are pregnant, not with a child but with a dream. You, too, are becoming fearful because the dream that was once active has grown still. Let me encourage you that sometimes things grow calm not because things are wrong but because things are right on schedule. It is the stillness alerting you that the dream growing inside you is preparing itself to be delivered.

There is a day coming when your dream will outgrow your womb.

God doesn't give us dreams for them to remain trapped within us. He graciously lets us conceive them and carry them

There is a day
coming when your
dream will outgrow
your womb.

for a season. When it is time for our dreams to be born, our dreams will send us signs that it's time for them to be released.

Many have asked, "How do I know *when* to birth my dream?"

My reply is, "When you have nothing left to give and there is no room for your dream to grow."

The truth is, your dream will let you know when it has outgrown your womb. There will be a day when your dream grows too big to remain on the inside of you. Your dream will position itself to break free from the environment of your womb. Not because it doesn't need you, but because it wasn't created to live inside you. Just like a baby in the womb, every dream will eventually seek out a larger environment. Dreams are created to be an extension of you, not to die within you.

I have a friend who was devastated when her business grew into the international market. While most people would be ecstatic about seeing their dream flourish, she went through a cycle of depression. When we talked through what she was feeling and why, we uncovered the root of her fears. The successful way in which her business was running made her feel unnecessary. A fledgling company once dependent on her every decision and oversight was now a healthy corporation led by an executive board. Just like women who experience postpartum depression after delivering their babies, my friend was feeling the same emotions following the growth of her business.

As women, we must get comfortable with our calling to carry and release things God places within our wombs. We've been created with the glorious ability to touch heaven and release prophetic promises into the world. It is with great awe that I consider our gender was created to conceive and carry life. It's time we take ownership of how we've been gifted.

FOR

1. Have you ever been in a storm where it seemed as though the winds were hitting you from every direction? How did you fare? Did your faith nearly buckle under the pressure, or did you face the storm boldly and stand on God's Word until the storm subsided?

2. Carrying that a step further, what advice would you give to a storm-ravaged friend whose life seems to be falling apart? What stories of your own might you share with that friend? What words of faith would you encourage her to embrace and to speak daily over her situation?

3. Has there ever been a time when it seemed as if God was wanting you to let go of something or someone you loved? Are you in that place now? If so, what is it that you're clutching so tightly even though you know it's time to let go? What are you afraid will happen if you let go?

4. Do you know someone who needs to let go of something but is resisting with all that's within her? What words of encouragement can you give her to help her release that person, thing, or dream to God?

TWELVE

WILD IMAGINATION

Every dream has a beginning. For Moses, it began in a field—watching his father-in-law's sheep.

Yawn. It was a job anyone could do but no one wanted to. Feed sheep. Watch sheep. Protect sheep. Chase after sheep. There were long seasons where nothing significant happened in the life of Moses. Four decades, to be exact.

I've often wondered, what does a person *do* when there's nothing to do?

> It's not easy to work on someone else's dream while yours is falling flat.
> It's depressing to watch the world move forward while you're sandwiched between seasons.
> It hurts to watch a friend's dreams play out on prime time while yours creeps along.

I'm sure you and I could have a large cup of coffee and talk about what it's like to *feel forgotten* by God. It's painful to watch our dreams turn into nightmares as we wait for something—*anything*—to happen. It's easy to grow impatient when we spend time doing the unimportant. We push hard to push open doors because we want out of the season we're in. We pray longer prayers in hopes they will be answered sooner rather than later. We spend our energy looking for a way out instead of looking up. If we don't learn how to deal with our impatience, we will end up with things God never intended us to have.

I had a friend who pulled open doors that God had pushed shut. I'm not sure if she was just tired of being stuck or if she feared others would move forward without her. Whatever her reasons were, she went against the wishes of her financial advisors and purchased a business that went belly-up the first year.

We live in a quick-fix culture. Our nature is to want things now. I'm curious to know, if it's our nature to live impatiently, why does God give us clues to our future? Why give us prophetic promises if we are going to make messes of them while we wait? In fact, why does He make us wait at all?

Maybe God uses the seasons we find most unfulfilling to fill us with a higher calling.

He may need to empty out our hearts so He can pour in our purpose.

Most of the heavenly assignments I've been given have come in seasons when God forced me to sit still. Maybe God deals with you the same way. If you are in a season in which nothing seems to be happening, use that time to be still and listen . . . listen carefully for the next instruction.

Moses was definitely still. Stone still.

Somewhere during the gazillionth year of watching sheep, Moses experienced something supernatural.

Take a moment and read through this account from Exodus with me:

> One day Moses was taking care of Jethro's flock. . . . The angel of the LORD appeared to him in flames of fire coming out of a bush. Moses saw that the bush was on fire, but it was not burning up. So he said, "I will go closer to this strange thing. How can a bush continue burning without burning up?"
>
> When the LORD saw Moses was coming to look at the bush, God called to him from the bush, "Moses, Moses!" And Moses said, "Here I am."
>
> Then God said, "Do not come any closer. Take off your sandals, because you are standing on holy ground." . . . Moses covered his face because he was afraid to look at God.
>
> The LORD said, "I have seen the troubles my people have suffered in Egypt, and I have heard their cries. . . . I will bring them out of that land and lead them to a good land with lots of room. . . . I am sending you to the king of Egypt. Go! Bring my people, the Israelites, out of Egypt!"
>
> But Moses said to God, "I am not a great man! How can I go to the king and lead the Israelites out of Egypt?" . . .
>
> The LORD said to him, "What is that in your hand?"
>
> Moses answered, "It is my walking stick."
>
> The LORD said, "Throw it on the ground."
>
> So Moses threw it on the ground, and it became a snake. Moses ran from the snake, but the LORD said to him, "Reach out and grab the snake by its tail." When Moses reached out and took hold of the snake, it again became a stick in his hand. (3:1–11; 4:2–4)

When I first read through this passage, I was shocked by Moses' hesitation to get on board with what God was doing. One would think, after a string of silent seasons, that Moses would welcome the opportunity to do something other than stare at sheep. Maybe that *was* the problem. He had spent so many years with sheep, he'd forgotten he wasn't one. It's easy to lose your identity when you're living without a purpose. The enemy of our souls doesn't always set traps to make us feel *uncomfortable*. Sometimes the trap is to make us *comfortable* in places we should never settle down in. *We grow roots when we should be growing wings.*

A college acquaintance spent months applying for her dream job—then turned down the job the day her application was accepted. A young lady in her twenties spent years auditioning for Broadway musicals until she finally landed a leading role—only to quit three months later. I could list others who, when given the opportunity to move forward, chose to stay stuck in their current situations.

When God appeared to Moses, Moses reacted in a similar way. God asked Moses to take on the role of a deliverer; he wanted to play the role of a shepherd.

Moses did his best to talk God out of using him:

> "I am not a great man! How can I go to the king and lead the Israelites out of Egypt? . . . What if the people of Israel do not believe me or listen to me? What if they say, 'The LORD did not appear to you'? . . . I have never been a skilled speaker. Even now, after talking to you, I cannot speak well. I speak slowly and can't find the best words." (Exodus 3:11; 4:1, 10)

Excuses, excuses. And worse, when God showed him the power He was making available to him by turning Moses' walking stick into a snake, "Moses ran from the snake" (4:3).

God had just performed a *miracle*, and Moses ran away.

One of the most dangerous things we can do in life is try to break *away* when God is trying to help us break *into*. God's next instruction to Moses was to go back to what he feared—the snake—and pick it up. In other words, confront what you fear.

Maybe you are in a situation like Moses' where God is calling you out of one place and sending you somewhere new. An abrupt move from the desert to a palace can make you feel off balance. Having your walking stick turn into a serpent isn't something you see every day either. When God begins to deal with us in ways we've never experienced, our reaction isn't always positive. Sometimes we, too, run away from our callings in fear.

Thankfully, God's grace allows us to practice using our faith when no one is watching. No crowd. No stage. No mic. He gives us warm-up moments on the side stage before handing us the mic on the main stage. Moses had his warm-up moment when God was the only one in the audience. It would make Moses more at home once he had a large audience, with everyone watching, and he'd have to act brave under pressure.

I cannot tell you the number of people who have walked away from their callings because they didn't want to act brave under pressure. They'd rather stay tucked away, nice and cozy, hiding their faith and not making waves.

God did not call us to hide our faith and live cozy, comfortable lives. He called us to be brave.

There are some brave actions that will be done quietly, but most will be lived out publicly. We cannot expect to be heroic and remain hidden.

In Matthew 5, Jesus gave this charge to the multitude following him:

> "You are the light of [Christ to] the world. A city set on a hill cannot be hidden; nor does *anyone* light a lamp and put it under a basket, but on a lampstand, and it gives light to all who are in the house. Let your light shine before men in such a way that they may see your good deeds *and* moral excellence, and [recognize and honor and] glorify your Father who is in heaven." (vv. 14–16 AMP)

See, rising to the challenge of accomplishing what we were created to do is not for our glory but for our Father's. If we are to honor Him, it's time we climb out of hiding and place our trust in His plan to fulfill our dreams and secure our futures.

I have an affinity for women who bravely defy the odds. And I enjoy celebrating those of our tribe who are willing to risk life and reputation to break boundaries and simply go for broke in response to their callings or in pursuit of their dreams. During the last few months I have enjoyed researching women who have flipped social expectations of our gender upside down. One of my favorite tales is from the early twentieth century. Legend records Annie Edson Taylor's story this way:

In 1901, on her sixty-third birthday, schoolteacher Annie

Taylor stuffed herself inside a mattress-padded oak pickle barrel and sailed over Niagara Falls. Nearly ninety minutes after being set adrift and plunging more than 150 feet, the top of Taylor's custom-made barrel was sawed off, and except for a few minor bumps and bruises, she emerged unscathed. That day, Taylor became the first person, male or female, to ride down Niagara Falls in a barrel. Her first words post-plunge: "No one ought ever do that again. I would sooner walk up to the mouth of a cannon, knowing it was going to blow me to pieces than make another trip over the fall."

> God did not call us to hide our faith and live cozy, comfortable lives. He called us to be brave.

"Why then, Ms. Taylor, did you face the falls?" a reporter asked her.

"My husband was killed in the Civil War, and I knew the fame of this feat would secure my financial future."

There you have it, women carving out ways to stay afloat. Yes, that's a pun. It's also a stark reality. But Taylor was willing to take a leap over the edge rather than wait to get pushed over the edge. How sad that she only performed her act of bravery because it was necessary for her survival. I hope we can turn the page and stop doing brave things simply because we fear something but rather because we want adventure.

In my study of what makes women do brave things, I have concluded that not all women who do brave things are brave. Sometimes certain situations will arise when women are forced to act with courage, but once the crisis is over, they revert to casual living and laid-back thinking. Braveheartedness should not be situational, and being a brave woman is not something you only do occasionally or when running away from something you fear. Bravehearted living is a daily decision, a resolve to move in the direction of your dreams. It is the willingness to confront those things that make you uncomfortable. It is refusing to stay stuck in situations that make you feel shameful. It is the courage to rise up when you would rather stay sitting down.

I knew a certain lady for more than twenty years. Every month or so our paths would cross and we would catch each other up on the details of our lives. After a while I began to notice a pattern in regard to how she dealt with life, or maybe I should say, how life dealt with her. When I would ask her, "How are things with you?" she would list off a string of negative situations that were overtaking her life. One month her problem was the IRS; the next month, an ex-husband; later on, her son was in jail; then she lost her job, and on the list could go. I had a feeling she lived life constantly on the run from things she didn't want to face or in fear of things she was forced to face.

Not once in twenty years did I hear her express interest in fulfilling a dream, pursuing a passion, or living out her purpose. I felt sorry for my friend. She never experienced the pleasure of diving into her future. The simple truth was, life led her around. And the places it took her were not the kind of scenic stops any of us would want to make.

Maybe you feel that way right now, as if you are being pulled through life without having any say in how things will go, and you're just barely hanging on, just trying to survive. Can I assure you, that is not how God designed you to go through life?

Bravehearted living is a
daily decision, a resolve
to move in the direction
of your dreams.

As God's daughters, we were created to thrive, and not only personally, but as a testimony to other women who could use an example. We were each meant to leave our mark on the earth. To make fresh footprints so other sisters can walk along a clear path. We have a responsibility to lead the way. To go first and pull back vines that would entangle our gender. To cut down the brush that would tear at our flesh and be thorns in our sides.

From one woman to another, I promise you: there is great reward for those who will make the sacrifice and clear the path for others to journey down. There is a hurting woman coming along behind you who needs you to cut some things out of her way. Without you she may lose sight of where she is going and wander down a dangerous path. Somewhere, there is a young girl searching for someone to take her by the hand and lead her away from doing something she will regret. And there is a sister so blinded by her emotions she can't see where to step next. Unless we sweep the path, she is in danger of sliding off a slope, and the fall may prove fatal.

> We were created to make fresh footprints so other sisters can walk along a clear path.

We are not to be held up by fear but to flourish so we can lead others in the faith.

The other day a friend called to tell me about an invitation she had received to do something that was on her dream list. In fact, it was something we had prayed over for years. When the opportunity to open a boutique franchise came available, it was a dream come true. Yet, my friend shied away in fear. By the time she called to share the news, she made a miracle sound miserable.

Before letting her dig her pit of pity too deep, I interrupted and asked, "Are you really going to tear apart your dream just as it is coming together?" I reminded her of the hours of intercession that had gone ahead of this opportunity. I challenged her to stop listening to the voices of doubt and fear and stay focused on her future. This was her moment to lunge forward for things that had always seemed out of her reach.

Are you in a similar situation, ready to extinguish a dream that is just beginning to smolder?

There comes a time when we have to stop running *from* our fears and begin running *toward* our dreams, because if we don't, those dreams will evaporate and become nightmares. And speaking of nightmares . . .

Last year I experienced a series of recurring nightmares. They weren't the casual kind of bad dream; they were the *Nightmare on Elm Street*–type dreams. I tried to push them out of my mind by day, but each night the nightmares grew longer and darker. Before long I recognized the deep spiritual connection they had to a situation I was walking through. I called together my prayer team and asked them to agree with me concerning how to interpret the dreams. At that particular time, our ministry was growing in a new direction, and our team had spent many hours praying for divine guidance. It didn't take me long to realize there was a correlation between the dreams I carried in my heart and the dreams I was having each night.

During that season, I discovered that our dreams come from two distinct channels: the ones our subconscious creates and the warnings or revelations that are sent from God. I felt certain these nightmares were not sent by God. But I also sensed He was trying to show me something through my dreams. After much prayer, I connected the recurring nightmares to the anxiety I was experiencing over our ministry's move in a new direction. Anxiety was not only opening a door for night terrors; it was also blocking the dreams God was trying to send. After praying through the anxiety, the nightmares immediately stopped. Days later I had a beautiful dream in which God confirmed that we were on the right track with the decisions we had made. That dream affirmed our vision and brought me courage to lead with confidence.

Maybe you are at a crossroads of faith right now. Perhaps, like me, you've been clinging to a dream by day and facing the fight of your life at night. If that is you, I encourage you to hold on to the promises God has given you. Seal them tightly inside your heart. Don't allow the enemy to rob you of the future that is right in front of you. Be brave! Please never forget, dear sister, that you are royalty. From before time was measurable, God had mapped out a plan for your life. Your existence is not accidental. You were not a mistake someone made. Your Father in heaven lovingly, meticulously fitted you together for a far greater purpose than you can imagine.

FOR

Further Reflection

1. Have you, like Moses, been living through a season of sitting still, but now, at last, God has opened up an entirely new opportunity for you? Will you embrace that opportunity eagerly and run with it—or run *from* it, like Moses from the snake?

2. When have you been called to a task that, in reality, you could do—and might even be *made* for—but you made excuses out of intimidation and a fear of failure? Is it too late to act courageously and take on that task or that ministry? Or has the opportunity passed you by?

3. Moses was raised in a palace, probably trained to be a leader—but he ended up in a pasture, tending sheep. Have you been groomed for something great, but now you find yourself far away from your dreams or your calling? What steps can you take to arise out of that passive place? Do you have the courage?

4. Have you ever had a recurring bad dream, or do you currently have them? What might they mean—or have you even considered that? Do you think they are just products of your subconscious, or could they be a message of God concerning your life and your future? Have you prayed for an answer? If not, will you?

chapter THIRTEEN

BRAVE:
THE NEW NORMAL

Many years ago, I stood at the basin of a capsule-shaped mountain table rising high above the desert floor. As I admired the lofty fortress, someone whispered, "That, dear one, is Masada. Its secrets are discoverable only by those willing to tempt fate and make the climb." Inquisitively, I glanced at the messenger, then back at the mountain. Both seemed intimidating.

Nearing 400 meters below sea level, Masada is one of the lowest points on earth. As I surveyed the terrain, I knew the 450-meter climb to the top would be a treacherous trek. Our guide informed us that there is only a narrow pathway to the top, not wide enough for two people to climb together. Each climber must ascend the winding path alone. Out of our group of fifty, only two men and I were daring enough to take on the risk. I was determined to make the climb because I wanted to know the mysteries that lay on that mountain.

Hours into the climb, I noticed that the higher we ascended, the more out of reach the summit appeared. Jagged rocks outlined the cliffs, and the desert fortress seemed impenetrable. If the cliffs weren't intimidating enough, the footpath certainly was. Only inches wide, the ancient passage didn't leave room for missteps. Even now I remember the sound loose stones made as they slid from beneath my feet and tumbled off the mountain.

As we neared the top of the stone table, my water reserve ran dry and my legs wobbled like a newborn giraffe's. I prayed the secrets of this fortress would be worth the risk to discover them.

There to greet us was an aged man dressed in a sandy-colored tunic. Hands outstretched, he said, "Masada welcomes you." Turning away, he motioned for us to follow him. During the next few hours we journeyed back in time and retraced the history of the glorious mountain. I will be a good friend and restrain myself from retelling the entire history of this archaic site. There is, however, one story that I must not fail to share.

Historian Flavius Josephus documented the only record we have of Masada. According to Josephus, Herod, the Roman king of Judea, built the fortress Masada as a place of refuge during the Roman occupation of Jerusalem. Seventy-five years after Herod's death, a group of Jewish zealots overtook the Roman garrison at Masada. For more than three years, the zealots raided and plundered the Roman camps in revolt against the occupation of Jerusalem.

In 73 CE, weary of the zealots' raids, Roman governor Flavius Silva marched against Masada. The Romans ascended the mountain, battering ram in tow, and laid siege to the mountain-top fortress, setting off "a volley of blazing torches . . . against a wall of timber."[1] The zealots realized that the Roman battering ram and catapults would succeed in breaching Masada's walls. Their leader, Elazar, resolved that the Jewish defenders should sacrifice their lives rather than surrender to Roman dictatorship.

As the Roman army advanced, Elazar gave a riveting, final speech to the Jewish defenders:

> Since we long ago resolved never to be servants to the Romans, nor to any other than to God Himself, Who alone is the true and just Lord of mankind, the time is now come that obliges us to make that resolution true in practice . . . We were the very first that revolted, and we are the last to fight against them; and I cannot but esteem it as a favor that God has granted us, that it is still in our power to die bravely, and in a state of freedom.

The story of Masada survived in the writings of Josephus, but for well over fifteen hundred years it was a forgotten episode in Jewish history. The story and its dramatic end remind us of the determination of the Jewish people to *live free* and *die bravely.*

To *live free* and *die bravely* is not an archaic mantra but a heart cry that is going forth from this generation. More than anything, the men and women of this present day want to be free and want their lives to count. Yet, as I travel throughout countries of the world, I hear the groanings of good, well-meaning people who've been lured to sleep by a spirit of mediocrity. It's time to wake them from their slumber. Many are willing to arise. But few have someone caring enough to set the alarm and stir them from their spiritual sleepiness.

As women of faith, we have been commissioned by God to awaken the souls of our sisters.

As a parent, it was my job to make sure our children were awake and prepared for school each day. Three of our children were easy to rouse. Getting the fourth up was an act of war. When I use the term *war*, that is exactly what I mean. It was warfare of the soul to pull her from the comfort of her warm bed. I admit there were days it would have been easier to let her continue her effortless dreaming. After all, she looked *sooo* beautiful resting. Many days I questioned, "Why should I break the spell and awaken her to the fractured and fallen world she will encounter all day long?"

Sounding the alarm for those who are ready to embrace life with confidence and courage is effortless. Being responsible to help those who have fallen into a deeper slumber and don't wish to be stirred requires a real commitment. And it requires bravery. But when you love someone deeply, you are not afraid to agitate her flesh by sounding an alarm. You're afraid that *not* stirring her will destroy any chance she might have for an adventurous life.

Not everything that entices us away from God's perfect plan appears evil. Sometimes the trap that is set is simply . . . comfortable. But it is a trap nonetheless, and it is the trap of complacency that most easily lures our souls away from the abundant life that God would have us live. We've all found

As women of faith,

we have been

commissioned by

God to awaken the

souls of our sisters.

ourselves stuck in seasons we would rather sleep through. The dangerous part of spiritual apathy is that we are not usually aware we are drifting from what God is calling us to do. Floating through life can take us in a direction far off the path of our dreams and our callings.

One day at the lake, I failed to anchor my boat correctly. After sleeping in the sun for a few hours, I woke to tree branches tangled in my sails. I was in a real mess, and it took a good portion of the day to untangle myself.

If we are honest, sometimes it takes a *mess* for us to get the *message* that we have floated off course. And sometimes we need a friend who is courageous enough to wake us from where we've wandered. I don't presume to know the circumstances you are walking through. But I do know what it feels like to wake up far from where I should be.

Not everyone who drifts away from their destiny does something immoral. It's just as easy to get off course doing good things, but not the best things; nice things but not dream-*filling* things, convenient things but not God-designed things—or nothing at all. How far we drift from our dreams and our purpose isn't always measurable by a moral compass.

The point is, it will take commitment to turn things around and go in the right direction. At those times, when I find myself adrift, I am reminded of God's grace to rescue us from the pitiful choices we sometimes make. If you've ever been lost and had your father come look for you, then you understand a taste of the endless love our Father has for His daughters. He doesn't stand by and wait for us to swim to shore. No, He plunges into the water and walks out to find us. He doesn't want us to stay trapped in our status quo. He wants us to live free.

⌒

Our messy, complicated lives are no challenge for our Creator. He won't turn you away if you have fallen into a sticky situation or done something that has caused damage to your life. His heart is to restore you to your rightful place. God's plan from the very beginning has been to cover your weaknesses and to showcase your confidence and courage. When the first woman found herself cloaked in nothing but shame, God sewed together a garment and placed it on her shoulders. He is still in the garment-making business; He just no longer uses animal skins. Instead He cloaks us with courage.

The thing about courage is, the longer you wear it, the more comfortably it fits. Like an oft-worn Italian shoe, it begins to gently take shape around our lives. Suddenly, you're not afraid anymore. You're willing to step out in faith and try new things. You're excited to take on new tasks that you may have been too intimidated to try before. You're ready to pursue your dreams and fulfill your callings. You're ready to make brave the new normal.

I'm discovering that more and more of God's daughters are finding the courage to make brave the new normal. They're

> God's plan from the very beginning has been to cover your weaknesses and to showcase your confidence and courage.

making waves and they're making a statement. As a result, their voices—our voices—are finally being heard.

For decades, even centuries, we have kept silent while our sisters have suffered. I'm not only referring to civil rights issues but matters of the heart. We have tribes of women around the world waiting on us to share words we've received from heaven, words that will launch them in a new direction. God's Word isn't the only thing He uses to convey His message. He uses women to better the lives of other women.

I can tell you from experience that while men may influence our lives, it is women who will shape our destinies. Men don't birth women. Women birth women. And women *help* women. If you are lacking in courage today, God, in His goodness, will link you with a woman who can help you put on the garment of courage and wear it well.

Now let's talk some more about how to wear the garment of courage.

Yesterday, I stumbled upon a blog post about the top ten fashion mistakes women over thirty make. Number seven nailed it for women close to my age: "Wearing too many accessories at one time will make you look cheap and outdated." The world's most elegant woman, Coco Chanel, was said to have offered this advice: "Before you leave the house, look in the mirror and take one thing off."[2]

Maybe that is good advice when it comes to wearing our courage. We are on a journey to becoming brave. We all want brave to be our new normal. But in pursuing a life lived with courage, we want to look bold but not brash. Some "accessories" are unbefitting for even the bravest of us. Mouthiness. Profanity. Bossiness. I've watched women leaders do more damage in a boardroom than men. Confidence is one thing, but coming across as overly confident and even arrogant can push everything we've tried to bring to the table right *off* the table. Courage should carry with it a certain elegance and dignity. There are few things less appealing than a bossy woman with a dirty mouth. If we want our words to carry weight, we need to frame them carefully.

In a world where our gender is encouraged to settle back and take second place, it is comforting to know there are women, like you, who are bravely rising up and taking charge of their futures. Today I set aside time to pray for your courage. I realize the journey to stepping out of the shadows of fear and heartache is no easy feat. It takes great effort and energy to push beyond a safe zone to pursue life with passion.

Living an enjoyable and fulfilling life begins with the determination to think big, walking in faith rather than fear. With worry and apprehension coursing through society, we must be intentional about guarding our hearts against anxiety and focusing instead on God's promises. Staying securely hidden in the words of our Father will keep us from becoming paralyzed, too nervous to take the next big step. The enemy's goal is to minimize our confidence,

> Courage should carry with it a certain elegance and dignity. If we want our words to carry weight, we need to frame them carefully.

to drown out our desire to *think big* and *dream wild*. But this is not the time to drown in a pool of hesitation or to be swept away by the current of cares. This is your season to swim into deeper waters and make brave your new normal.

Right now, I am thinking about the journey before you. How I wish I were able to spend time hearing your story and talking you through the process of becoming brave. But while we may never meet in person, the Holy Spirit has already connected our hearts. And I believe that the moments we have shared together in this book are the starting point of a long, beautiful friendship. In the days to come, I look forward to hearing how your faith has grown. I believe there is so much joy God wants to bring to your heart, and I can't wait to hear of the adventures that are sure to become a part of your life's story.

As we end this journey we have taken together—your journey to becoming *brave*—I hope you know how deeply I care for you. I appreciate your enthusiasm for opening your heart to God's Word and the message He has given me to pass on to you. I will think about you and pray for you with great love and affection. Meanwhile, as we say goodbye to each other—for now—let me offer this prayer for you:

> [As I] get down on my knees before the Father, this magnificent Father who parcels out all heaven and earth[,] I ask him to strengthen you by his Spirit—not a brute strength but a glorious inner strength—that Christ will live in you as you open the door and invite him in. And I ask him that with both feet planted firmly on love, you'll be able to take in with all followers of Jesus the extravagant dimensions of Christ's love. Reach out and

experience the breadth! Test its length! Plumb the depths! Rise to the heights! Live full lives, full in the fullness of God. (Ephesians 3:16–19 THE MESSAGE)

Now *go*. Be brave. And yes, live free in the fullness of God.

1. Is there a Masada-like "mountain" that you are wanting to climb—say, a dream you'd like to pursue or an invitation you'd like to explore—but trepidation has kept you from taking that first step? What excuses are you making to avoid moving forward? Is there any validity to them, or are they *just* excuses? What would it take for you to resolve to put the first foot forward?

2. Who do you know who needs a wake-up call, specifically, someone who just needs the courage to get out of a stagnant place, or even a dangerous place, and begin moving in a new direction? Are you brave enough to sound the alarm? If not, wouldn't you hope she would do the same for you?

3. Think about the bravest, most confident woman you know, someone who made a daring move and succeeded. Was she always so confident? Did her success come easy? Or did it take courage to overcome her fears and defy overwhelming odds to get where she is today? Do you find yourself admiring her, or envying her?

4. Thinking further about this same courageous woman, what are some of the "accessories" she wears along with her garment of courage—that is, what are some of her traits? Is she brash, or simply honest? Direct, or just plain mouthy? More important, is she a woman of class and dignity whom you'd be proud to emulate? What makes her so brave?

BRAVE QUOTES

Chapter 1: Join the Ranks

A victorious life is not stumbled upon; it is cultivated. It's the result of choosing to be bold, brave—*fearless*— when everything in you wants to cower in defeat.

Think big, dream wild, and live fear-free!

Chapter 2: Wired to Be Brave

The journey to becoming brave usually lands us at the intersection of indecision and determination.

The world is after what makes us most like God. By divine design we are wired to be redeemers and warriors.

It is time for the daughters of destiny to rise up and pray risky prayers that force hell to tremble.

Chapter 3: Changing Your Trajectory

Don't stop dreaming the moment it gets daring.

God loves answering prayers of faith, performing the
impossible, and fulfilling His daughters' secret dreams.

Uniting women in a culture that pits us
against each other is a tall order.

People of faith don't always start out fearless; sometimes
the worrier has to evolve into a warrior.

Chapter 4: The Flashing Blade

You can be both feminine and fierce. One
doesn't cancel the other out.

But as daughters of the King, our roles as heroines aren't optional.
They are engraved in our heritage and inscribed in our destinies.

If you're longing for approval, don't look around, look up.

Chapter 5: A Dream Thief

Betrayal is the number one tactic the
enemy uses to steal our courage.

If our enemy cannot get us to lay down our swords in
frustration, he will get us to turn them on each other.

It is not uncommon for friends to turn into rivals
the moment dreams begin to flourish.

Chapter 6: More Than a Spartan

God has an epic role for each of us to
play, even you. The question is, are you
willing to show up for the audition?

What we continue to confess will become
the framework of our future.

Bravehearted people have a way of empowering
the timid to face giants that look terrifying.

Chapter 7: The Quest

It takes a great deal of nerve to love
someone who betrays our trust.

How different would the journey be if we
chose to defend and protect one another rather
than expose one another's vulnerabilities?

Chapter 8: It's All About Timing

If we are not intentional about mapping out our
dreams, someone will map them out for us.

Although the enemy cannot read your
mind, he can read your reactions.

Frustration occurs the moment we
put our present circumstances up
against supernatural promises.

Chapter 9: Capturing Your Courage

What personal crisis would you make public if you
knew it would make your sisters stronger?

What we hide in our hearts during secure seasons will make
our hearts strong and our words sound during stormy seasons.

When we are comfortable with doing the illogical,
God can perform the unpredictable.

Chapter 10: God's Silence, Our Words

We must learn to listen to what He is saying
when He is saying nothing at all.

Sometimes God will ask us to do things that
make us feel more fragile than fearless.

When someone picks a fight, don't
always reach for your sword.

Chapter 11: Stormy Seasons

God never shortchanges His daughters.

There is a day coming when your dream
will outgrow your womb.

Chapter 12: Wild Imagination

God did not call us to hide our faith and live cozy,
comfortable lives. He called us to be brave.

Bravehearted living is a daily decision, a resolve
to move in the direction of your dreams.

We were created to make fresh footprints so
other sisters can walk along a clear path.

Chapter 13: Brave: The New Normal

As women of faith, we have been commissioned
by God to awaken the souls of our sisters.

God's plan from the very beginning has
been to cover your weaknesses and to
showcase your confidence and courage.

Courage should carry with it a certain elegance
and dignity. If we want our words to carry
weight, we need to frame them carefully.

NOTES

Chapter 2: Wired to Be Brave

1. Mimi Haddad, "Ideas Have Consequences," *Red Letter Christians*, June 16, 2011, https://www.redletterchristians.org/ideas-have-consequences/.
2. Chana Weisberg, "Can a Change of Name Create a Change of Destiny?," *TheJewishWoman.org* (blog), accessed January 15, 2018, http://www.chabad.org/theJewishWoman/article_cdo/aid/2235035/jewish/Can-a-Change-of Name-Create-a-Change-of-Destiny.htm.

Chapter 4: The Flashing Blade

1. *Wonder Woman*, directed by Patty Jenkins, written by Allan Heinberg (Burbank, CA: Warner Bros., 2017).
2. Amanda Cook, "You Make Me Brave," *You Make Me Brave: Live at the Civic*, Bethel Music, 2014, album, https://www.azlyrics.com/lyrics/bethelmusic/youmakemebrave.html.

Chapter 6: More Than a Spartan

1. *300*, directed by Zack Snyder (Burbank, CA: Warner Bros., 2007).
2. Gretchen, "300 Movie Review: Spartan Women Shown Respect," https://www.girlscantwhat.com/300-movie-review-spartan-women-shown-respect/.
3. *Criminal Minds*, season 3, episode 5, "Seven Seconds," directed by John Gallagher, written by Andy Bushell, October 24, 2007, aired on CBS.

Chapter 7: The Quest

1. Andrea Mustain, "Tree Strangers: Vines Overtaking Tropical Forests," *Live Science*, April 5, 2011, https://www.livescience.com/30300-invasive-vines -lianas-tropical-rainforests.html.

2. Himanshu Sharma, October 20,1014, "10 Seemingly Impossible Things Made Possible By Science," https://listverse.com/2014/10/20/10 -seemingly-impossible-things-made-possible-by-science/.

Chapter 8: It's All About Timing

1. *Samurai Warrior Queens*, Smithsonian Channel documentary, https://www .smithsonianchannel.com/shows/samurai-warrior-queens/0/3420808.

2. Michaela Anchan, January 10, 2016, "Herstory: The Trung Sisters: Brave Heroines of Vietnamese History," https://www.connectedwomen.co /magazine/herstory-the-trung-sisters-brave-heroines-of-vietnamese-history/.

3. Pauli Poisuo, August 6, 2013, "10 Fascinating Facts About Samurai," https://www.smithsonianchannel.com/shows/samurai-warrior-queens/0 /3420808.

Chapter 9: Capturing Your Courage

1. "My Brain Surgery Filmed from My Perspective," YouTube video, 11:36, posted by Courtelizz1, June 28, 2017, https://www.youtube.com/watch ?time_continue=471&v=mwOzsxaMfM0.

Chapter 10: God's Silence, Our Words

1. Olivia Peay, "The Expedition (Lewis, Clark, and Sacagawea)," https://sites .google.com/a/uconn.edu/oap10004/home/introduction/origins-of-the -expedition/the-expedition-lewis-clark-and-sacagawea.

Chapter 13: The New Normal

1. I. A. Richmond, "The Roman Siege-Works of Masada, Israel," *Journal of Roman Studies* 52 (1962): 142–55, doi:10.2307/297886.

2. "The Most Inspiring Coco Chanel Quotes to Live By," *Vogue*, August 20, 2015, https://www.vogue.com.au/fashion/news/the-most-inspiring-coco-chanel -quotes-to-live-by/image-gallery/b1cb17be7e20734d0b255fbd5a478ed4?pos=1.

ABOUT THE
AUTHOR

Tracey Mitchell is an international speaker, author of the inspirational *Downside Up*, executive producer and TV host of *Life
from DFW*, CEO of the Winning Woman Consulting Group,
host of the Thrive Women's Conference, and vice president
of Christian Women in Media Association. Her love of life is
evident, as is her passion for Christ and compassion for hurting
people. Living in Dallas, Texas, Tracey is a wife and mom.

Also by Tracey

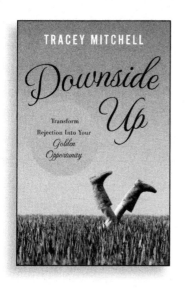

Downside Up: Transforming Rejection into Your Golden Opportunity

The Invitation: Intimacy with the Father

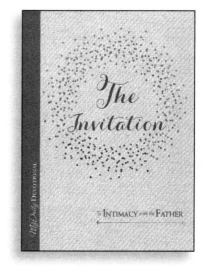

Power House Photography, Carmela Lynn

WEBSITE:
traceymitchell.com

FACEBOOK:
officialtraceymitchell

TWITTER:
traceymitchell1

INSTAGRAM:
Tracey Mitchell